IMPLEMENTING IT GOVERNA

Other publications by Van Haren Publishing

Van Haren Publishing (VHP) specializes in titles on Best Practices, methods and standards within four domains:
- IT management
- Architecture (Enterprise and IT)
- Business management and
- Project management

Van Haren Publishing offers a wide collection of whitepapers, templates, free e-books, trainer material etc. in the **VHP Knowledge Base**: www.vanharen.net for more details.

VHP is also publisher on behalf of leading organizations and companies:
ASLBiSL Foundation, CA, Centre Henri Tudor, Gaming Works, Getronics, IACCM, IAOP, IPMA-NL, ITSqc, NAF, Ngi, PMI-NL, PON, Quint, The Open Group, The Sox Institute, Tmforum.

Topics are (per domain):

IT (Service) Management / IT Governance	Architecture (Enterprise and IT)	Project/Programme/ Risk Management
ABC of ICT	Archimate®	A4-Projectmanagement
ASL	GEA®	ICB / NCB
BiSL	SOA	MINCE®
CATS CM®	TOGAF®	M_o_R®
CMMI		MSP™
CoBIT	**Business Management**	P3O®
Frameworx	Contract Management	*PMBOK® Guide*
ISO 17799	EFQM	PRINCE2®
ISO 27001	eSCM	
ISO 27002	ISA-95	
ISO/IEC 20000	ISO 9000	
ISPL	ISO 9001:2000	
IT Service CMM	OPBOK	
ITIL®	Outsourcing	
ITSM	SAP	
MOF	SixSigma	
MSF	SOX	
SABSA	SqEME®	

For the latest information on VHP publications, visit our website: www.vanharen.net.

Implementing IT Governance
A Pocket Guide

Dr Gad J Selig PMP COP

Van Haren
PUBLISHING

Colophon

Title:	Implementing IT Governance: A Pocket Guide
Author:	Dr Gad J Selig PMP COP
Publisher:	Van Haren Publishing, Zaltbommel, www.vanharen.net
ISBN:	978 90 8753 216 1
Edition:	First edition, first impression, June 2008
	First edition, second impression, October 2011
Design and Layout:	CO2 Premedia bv, Amersfoort -- NL
Printer:	Wilco, Amersfoort-NL

© 2008 Van Haren Publishing

For any further enquiries about Van Haren Publishing, please send an e-mail to: info@vanharen.net

Preface

Information Technology (IT) has become an integral part of many organizations and is fundamental to sustain business growth, innovation and transformation and support continuing operations in most organizations. Information Technology and its effective management is a fundamental cornerstone of any well-run business. Insuring that this cornerstone is optimized is all about optimizing the business side of IT. IT governance is vital to the success of the IT function within corporate enterprises on a global basis.

The purpose of the pocket guide is to provide a comprehensive checklist for the Board, executives, managers and most of all, CIOs and IT professionals. It provides a guideline to use in any organization and in any industry to formulate and tailor an effective approach to IT governance and to help transition the IT organization to a higher level of business/ IT alignment, maturity, effectiveness, and value creation function for an organization. It is derived from the book entitled, "Implementing IT Governance – A Practical Guide to Global Best Practices in IT Management" published by Van Haren Publishing.

This title lays out a roadmap to executing within a comprehensive governance framework. It provides a comprehensive checklist that will help the board, executive management and, most of all, CIOs and IT professionals, think through what has worked, what can work and how to plan and deploy IT governance successfully. The pocket guide provides a summary checklist of all of the key components and critical success factors to make IT governance real, effective and sustainable. It represents a valuable resource for all business and IT practitioners, and brings together every critical aspect relating to IT management and governance.

The book reinforces the fact that IT cannot run as an independent silo. It must be aligned and integrated properly with the business and all facets of the organization. It represents an excellent instructional supplement, as well as a thorough source of reference. Each topic has a very detailed list of informational details. It is a must-have for every executive or manager who deals with IT, as well as every professor teaching business and IT courses. The full details of all material referenced in this Pocket Guide are found in the main title: Implementing IT Governance ISBN: 9789087531195

Acknowledgements

I gratefully acknowledge the help and support of a number of individuals, organizations and their members in the private, public and academic sectors, in conducting the research, editing the book, participating in developing the case studies, allowing me to consult for and/or teach them, and influencing, reinforcing and validating the findings, recommendations, critical success factors and lessons learned.

I would like to thank specific people for their help, contributions and insights: Michael Pellegrino of FujiFilm USA, Jaci Coleman of Peoples United Bank, Christine Bullen at Stevens Institute of Technology, Neal Bronzo of Pepsi Bottling Company, Stuart Werner at Li and Fung, USA, Kevin Laing at ATMI, Paul Bateman at AXA, Peter Waterhouse and Debra Cattani at CA, Charles Popper at the TechPar Group, Rebecca Brunotti, formerly of the General Services Administration – Federal Technology Services, Joann Martin at Pitney Bowes, Joseph Puglisi at EMCOR, Len Peters at Columbia Business School, Porter Sherman at UBS, Hank Zupnick at GE Real Estate, Sigal Zarmi of GE Commercial Finance, Nicholas Willcox at Unilever, Mike Bodetti at TNT Expense Management, Tarek Sobh, Ward Thrasher and Robert Todd at the University of Bridgeport, Michael Corbett at IAOP, Jane Siegel at ITsqc, Dick Lefave at Sprint Nextel, Peter Shay at TAC, Jim Shay at Syracuse University, Erran Carmel at American University and many others.

Special thanks go to Omur Yilmaz and Sujani Pradhan, my graduate assistants at the University of Bridgeport, who helped me with conducting research for the book and co-ordinating the many revisions to the manuscript. I also want to thank the many executives, managers and professionals who have attended my seminars and workshop over the years, as well my students who have attended my graduate classes. All of them have contributed to my knowledge and challenged me to learn more and stay current in a rapidly changing field.

In addition, I would like to thank my publisher, Annelise Savill at Van Haren Publishing for her friendship, editorial suggestions and encouragement to complete this project, as well as my editor, Jayne Wilkinson.

I would like to dedicate this book to my wife, mate and life-long partner, Phyllis, for her love, dedication, understanding and support that she has given me throughout our time together. Our children, Camy, Dan, Gabe, our children through marriage, Beth and Andy, and our grandchildren, Jason, Jacob, and Jesse, also inspired me to finish the project, so that I could devote more time to them. I would most of all dedicate this book to my mother, Ruth, who passed away in November 2007, without whom this project would not have been possible.

Dr Gad J Selig
May 2008

About the Author

Dr Gad J Selig is the Director, Masters of Science in Technology Management and Dual Graduate Business and Engineering Degree Programs, and leads the Center for Inter-disciplinary Business, Engineering and Technology Leadership at the University of Bridgeport.

Dr Selig is also the Managing Partner of GPS Group, Inc., a consulting, research and education firm that focuses on strategic marketing and growth, business and technology transformation, IT strategy and governance, program/project management, strategic sourcing and innovation and managing change.

Dr Selig has more than thirty years of diversified domestic/international executive, management and consulting experience, with both Fortune 500 and smaller companies in the financial services, utility, telecommunications, software and high technology, manufacturing and retail industries. His experience includes: marketing, sales, planning, operations, business development, mergers and acquisitions, general management (with full P & L responsibility), systems/network integration, strategic sourcing and outsourcing, MIS/CIO, electronic commerce, product development, project management, business process transformation, governance and entrepreneurship. Dr Selig has worked for the following companies: Marketing Corporation of America, Advanced Networks and Services, Continental Group, Contel Information Systems, NYNEX (Verizon), Standard Kollsman Industries, CBS and AT&T.

He earned degrees from City, Columbia and Pace Universities in Economics, Engineering and Business. He has authored three books and over 50 refereed articles and/or conference proceedings. He is a dynamic and popular speaker at industry conferences in the U.S. and abroad.

Dr Selig has been a board member of Telco Research, BIS Group, LTD. and AGS. He is a member of the Academy of Management, Project Management Institute, IAOP, ISACA and others. He holds a top secret clearance with the U.S. Federal Government.

Dr Gad J Selig PMP COP
Director, Technology Management & Dual Graduate Business/Engineering Degree Programs, University of Bridgeport, Graduate Schools of Business and Engineering &
Managing Partner, GPS Group, Inc.
E-mail: gjselig@optonline.net
www.gpsgroupinc.com

Table of contents

Pocket Guide

Chapter 1
Introduction to IT/business alignment, planning, execution and governance

1.1   Overview

The issues, opportunities and challenges of aligning information technology more closely with an organization, and effectively governing an organization's information technology (IT) investments, resources, major initiatives and superior uninterrupted service, is becoming a major concern of the Board and executive management in enterprises on a global basis. Information technology (IT) has become a vital function in most organizations, and is fundamental to support and sustain innovation and growth.

Therefore, a comprehensive top-down approach, with bottom-up execution of IT governance, which includes all the activities of business/ IT alignment, planning, execution and governance of IT, as well as the leadership of those entrusted with the task, is critical to achieve a cost effective solution. Effective 'management' includes the activities of planning, investment, integration, measurement and deployment, and providing the services required to manage a complex strategic asset.

None of this is easy, or obvious, and this pragmatic and actionable 'how to' pocket guide is intended to draw from about 200 current and emerging best practice sources, and over twenty IT governance best practice case studies.,

1.1.1   Major challenges and issues faced by IT

In our research, we compiled a list of IT challenges and issues, identified by multiple independent sources. There appears to be a common thread running through these issues and therefore, we have summarized them into strategic, value enhancing and execution questions.

Board and executive questions for IT:
- Does the IT strategy align with the business strategy?
- Is the IT investment justified, based on its contributions to the business?
- How likely will IT meet or exceed its plans, objectives and initiatives?
- Is IT being managed prudently or effectively? How is it measured?
- How is IT delivering value? Is there a consistent IT business case format used for justifying IT investments?
- Is IT developing and maintaining constructive relationships with customers, vendors and others?
- Is IT delivering projects and services on time, within scope, within budget and with high quality?
- Is IT staffed adequately, with the right skills and competencies?
- Is there a standard measurement for IT investment across the firm?
- How does IT management and operations compare to other best practice organizations?
- How is IT managing and planning for contingencies, disasters, security, and back-up?
- How is IT measuring its performance? What are the key performance measures?
- How effectively is IT communicating its progress and problems to its constituents?
- What controls and documentation have been instituted in IT? Are they sufficient?
- Does the Board review and possibly approve the IT strategy?

- Is a risk management policy, assessment and mitigation practice followed for IT?
- Is IT compliant to federal, state, country (for global organizations) regulations, and to internal policies and controls?
- Are IT audit policies, procedures and processes in place and followed?
- Is there a succession plan in place for the CIO and key direct reports?

1.1.2 Summary of key strategic, value enhancing and execution questions:

Strategic questions - Are we doing the right thing?
Is the investment in IT:
- in line with our business vision and strategy? is the board and/or executive operating management involved and committed?
- consistent with our business principles, plan and direction?
- contributing to our strategic objectives, sustainable competitive differentiation and business continuity support?
- providing optimum value at an acceptable level of risk?
- representing a long-term view (roadmap)
- including an architectural roadmap, based on a detailed analysis of the current state or condition of IT?
- Does the CIO have a seat at the "C" table?

Value questions – Are we getting the benefits?
Is there:
- a clear and shared understanding and commitment to achieve the expected benefits? In what areas? How?
- clear accountability for achieving the benefits, which should be linked to MBOs and incentive compensation schemes, for individuals and business units, or functional areas?

Are they:

- based on relevant and meaningful metrics?
- based on a consistent benefits realization process and sign-off?

Delivery and execution questions – Are we deploying well and effectively? How do we measure our results?
Metrics include:

- scalable, disciplined and consistent management, governance, delivery of quality processes
- appropriate and sufficient resources available with the right competencies, capabilities and attitudes
- a consistent set (of metrics) linked to critical success factors (CSFs) and realistic key performance indicators (KPIs)
- succession planning

Major IT challenges must be dealt with as part of an IT planning and governance process

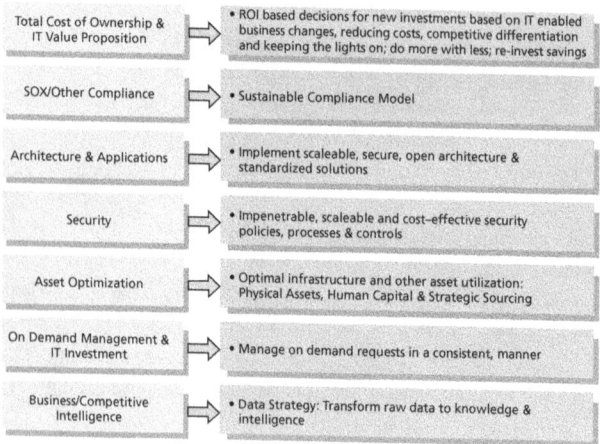

Total Cost of Ownership & IT Value Proposition	• ROI based decisions for new investments based on IT enabled business changes, reducing costs, competitive differentiation and keeping the lights on; do more with less; re-invest savings
SOX/Other Compliance	• Sustainable Compliance Model
Architecture & Applications	• Implement scaleable, secure, open architecture & standardized solutions
Security	• Impenetrable, scaleable and cost-effective security policies, processes & controls
Asset Optimization	• Optimal infrastructure and other asset utilization: Physical Assets, Human Capital & Strategic Sourcing
On Demand Management & IT Investment	• Manage on demand requests in a consistent, manner
Business/Competitive Intelligence	• Data Strategy: Transform raw data to knowledge & intelligence

Figure 1.1 Major challenges for IT

Figure 1.1 summarizes the major IT challenges being addressed by a large, global software organization, as part of its IT planning and governance process.

Basically, it comes down to the need for a plan that can be executed. At the same time, the role of the CIO is also undergoing significant change. Successful CIOs recognize that IT has become far more than a means of increasing efficiency and reducing costs. Rather, they see IT as a prime stimulus for, and enabler of, business innovation – and themselves as key collaborators in a process that develops business and IT strategies in unison.

1.2 Definition, purpose and scope of IT governance

Definition of IT governance:
Governance formalizes and clarifies oversight, accountability and decision rights for a wide array of IT strategy, resource and control activities. It is a collection of management, planning and performance review policies, practices and processes; with associated decision rights, which establish authority, controls and performance metrics over investments, plans, budgets, commitments, services, major changes, security, privacy, business continuity and compliance with laws and organizational policies.

Purpose of IT governance
IT governance:
- aligns IT investments and priorities more closely with the business
- manages, evaluates, prioritizes, funds, measures and monitors requests for IT services, and the resulting work and deliverables, in a more consistent and repeatable manner that optimize returns to the business
- maintains responsible utilization of resources and assets
- establishes and clarifies accountability and decision rights (clearly defines roles and authority)

- ensures that IT delivers on its plans, budgets and commitments
- manages major risks, threats, change and contingencies proactively
- improves IT organizational performance, compliance, maturity, staff development and outsourcing initiatives
- improves the voice of the customer (VOC), demand management and overall customer and constituent satisfaction and responsiveness
- manages and thinks globally, but acts locally
- champions innovation within the IT function and the business

Scope of IT Governance:

Key IT governance strategy and resource decisions must address the following topics: (Modified from Weill and Ross, 2004; Popper, 2000)

- **IT principles** – high level statements about how IT is used in the business (eg scale, simplify and integrate; reduce TCO (Total Cost of Operations) and self fund by re-investing savings; invest in customer facing systems; transform business and IT through business process transformation; strategic plan directions, PMO (project management office), sustain innovation and assure regulatory compliance, etc.)
- **IT architecture** – organizing logic for data, applications and infrastructure captured in a set of policies, relationships, processes, standards and technical choices, to achieve desired business and technical integration and standardization
- **SOA architecture** – service oriented architecture (SOA) is a business-centric IT architectural approach that supports the integration of the business as linked, repeatable business tasks or services; SOA helps users build composite applications that draw upon functionality from multiple sources within and beyond the enterprise to support business processes
- **IT infrastructure** – centrally co-ordinated, based on shared IT services that provide the foundation for the enterprise's IT capability and support

- **business application needs** – specifying the business need for
  purchased or internally developed IT applications
- **IT investment and prioritization** – decisions about how much and
  where to invest in IT (eg capital and expense), including development
  and maintenance projects, infrastructure, security, people, etc.
- **people (human capital) development** – decisions about how to
  develop and maintain global IT leadership management succession and
  technical skills and competencies (eg how much and where to spend
  on training and development, industry individual and organizational
  certifications, etc.)
- **IT governance policies, processes, mechanisms, tools and metrics**
  – decisions on composition and roles of steering groups, advisory
  councils, technical and architecture working committees, project teams;
  key performance indicators (KPIs); chargeback alternatives; performance
  reporting, meaningful audit process and the need to have a business
  owner for each project and investment

Successful IT governance is built on three critical pillars – leadership, organization and decision rights, scalable processes and enabling technologies

Effective IT governance is built on three critical pillars. These pillars
include: leadership, organization and decision rights, flexible and scalable
processes, and the use of enabling technology (Luftman, 2004; Board
Effectiveness Partners, 2004; Melnicoff, 2005; Pultorak and Kerrigan,
2005):

- **Leadership, organization and decision rights** - define the organization
  structure, roles and responsibilities, decision rights (decision influencers
  and makers), a shared vision and interface/integration touch points and
  champions for proactive change:
  - roles and responsibilities are well defined with respect to each of the

IT governance components and processes, including the steering and review hierarchies for investment authorizations, resolution of issues and formal periodic reviews

- clear hand-off and interface agreements and contracts exist for internal and external work and deliverables
- motivated leaders and change champions with the right talent, drive and competencies
- meaningful metrics
- CIO is a change agent who links process to technology within the business, and provides the tools for enablement and innovation

- **Flexible and scalable processes** - the IT governance model places heavy emphasis on the importance of process transformation and improvement: (eg planning, project management, portfolio investment management, risk management, IT Service Management and delivery, performance management, vendor management, controls and audits, etc.):
  - processes are well defined, documented, measured
  - processes define interfaces between organizations and ensure that workflow spans boundaries and silos including organization, vendors, geography, technology and culture
  - processes should be flexible, scalable and consistently applied, with common sense

- **Enabling technology** - leverage leading tools and technologies that support the major IT governance components:
  - processes are supported by software tools that support the IT imperatives and components (eg planning and budgeting, portfolio investment management, project management, risk and change management, IT Service Management and delivery processes, financial, asset and performance management and scorecards, etc.)
  - tools provide governance, communications and effectiveness metrics to accelerate decisions, follow-up and management actions

If any one of the above pillars is missing or ineffective, the IT governance initiative will not be effective or sustainable. In addition, over dependence on one dimension over the others will result in sub-optimal performance.

IT governance – decision rights and authority

Peter Weill and Jeane Ross (Weill and Ross, 2004) identified the concept of IT decision rights as an important component of effective IT governance. The purpose of a decision rights matrix is to identify the IT decision influencers and decision makers in an organization, to clarify the decision roles and authority levels for the major IT areas. It eliminates confusion, identifies accountability and clearly defines decision roles and scope.

Figure 1.2 provides an illustrative example of a partial IT governance decision rights matrix for a financial services organization.

IT/business steering and governance boards, working committees and roles

Many top performing companies have established multi-level and multi-disciplinary business/IT steering and governance boards and working committees, with clear roles and responsibilities, to ensure appropriate commitments, sponsorship, escalation, ownership, more effective communications and more formal visibility and commitment of the Board, executive management and other constituents.

Why are they important?
They:
- help to ensure alignment across all of the parts of an organization; it is recognized that the demand for IT resources will exceed available resources/budget, and establishing organization wide and business unit priorities is essential

A decisions rights matrix identifying decision influencers and decision makers is necessary to clarify decision roles and authority levels for the major It governance components

IT Governance Component	Input to Decision	Decision Authority	Comments/Examples (Varies by Organization)
IT Principles (High value statements about how IT will be used to create business value)	Business Units	IT Senior Leadership Group & CIO; Executive Officer Group	• Scale, simplify, integrate • Reduce cost of IT & self fund • Re-engineer/consistent processes • Invest in customer facing systems • Investment $ Threshold Approvals • Key Performance Indicators/CSFs
IT Investment, Plan, Prioritization, Critical Success Factors and Key Performance Indicators (KPIs)	Business Units	IT Steering Committee (ITSC) (Business & IT Executives), Projects over $500K:	• ITSC recommends priority to CEO for any projects requiring over $500K • Identify, track and measure critical success factors and associated KPIs
Business Applications	Business Units and Corporate Functional Unit Heads	IT Steering Committee	**Significant business application spend must be approved during the annual budget process, and if over $500K, approved by ITSC**
IT Infrastructure and Architecture; Outsourcing & Vendor Management; +++Others	IT Steering Committee IT Steering Committee + Business Units	IT Architecture/Technology Review Board (and Business Units (for related applications) Senior leadership (Depends on scope)	**Significant infrastructure spend must be approved during the annual budget process, and if over $500K, approved by ITSC. Significant outsourcing initiative should be recommended by ITSC & approved by Executive Officer Group**

Figure 1.2 IT governance decision rights (financial service organization)

- provide a forum for investment decision-making which is synchronized with the business
- build an enterprise view and help to eliminate stovepipe systems, processes, and duplication of effort across the organization

What (charter) should they focus on?

Boards should aim:

- to review and approve strategic plans, major programs/projects and establish priorities among competing requests for resources to ensure that everyone is aligned on those initiatives with highest 'value add' to the organization as a whole

- to establish and support processes where needed, to effectively fulfil the charge outlined
- to conduct formal periodic reviews of major initiatives, and operational service performance

Roles and responsibilities:

They:

- review and approve overall IT plans
- review, prioritize, approve major IT investments
- conduct formal periodic project progress and performance reviews
- final escalation point for major IT/business issues resolution
- support and sponsor IT governance policy and process improvement programs impacting the Executive Steering Board membership organizations, and help deploy them in their organizations

Other steering and working committees:

- Successful IT governance requires multi-level and multi-functional participation. Many organizations establish additional business/IT working committees at the business unit level, as well as major functional areas such as supply chain management, global financials, marketing and sales, research and development, and others as necessary.
- Program and projects working groups focus on specific initiatives.

Figure 1.3 illustrates an example of the IT/business steering and governance boards and roles at multiple levels for a large organization.

IT demand management - sources and classifications

Typically, requests for IT services should be identified and accommodated for in the strategic and tactical plans and budgets. If they are not, they are classified as 'out-of-plan'. Therefore, each request should be evaluated on its own merits against consistent evaluation criteria discussed in more detail in Chapter 3.

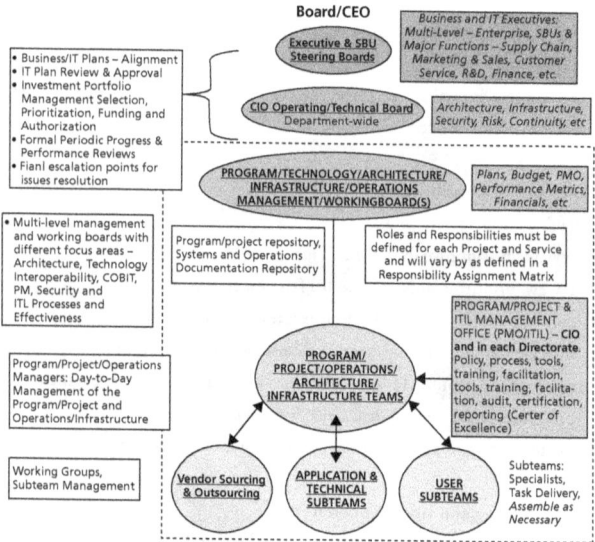

Figure 1.3 IT/business steering and governance boards, working committees and roles

Demand for IT services generally comes in several flavours — mandatory ('must do's' such as addressing service interruptions, standard maintenance, keeping the lights on and/or regulatory compliance) and discretionary ('could do's' if aligned, feasible, cost justified, strategic and/or requested by executive management). Both mandatory and discretionary requests should be approved by the business/IT leadership in the IT strategic and operating plans, or in accordance with an organization's decision rights and approval authority guidelines established for IT.

The following considerations will further help prioritize business needs with IT:

- clearly define and relate the value (eg cost reduction, containment and avoidance; increased revenues; faster access to information; shorter time

to market etc.) that IT provides in support of the business
- identify value adding activities (eg value chain and other business models/attributes) and strategies that would enhance then through IT.
- focus on listening to the voice of the customer
- ensure that all IT initiatives are evaluated using a consistent, but flexible set of investment selection, prioritization and review criteria, to assure a strong link to the business plan, project implementation and on-going operations
- develop a strategic IT plan that identifies major initiatives, technical/architecture, operational, organizational, people development and financial objectives and measurements in support of the business

Figure 1.4 illustrates a demand management chart for a major bank.

Classification	Type of Request or Demand Mgt.	Comments/Description
Mandatory or Core (Business Enablement)	Service Interruption (Break & Fix)	A problem caused the disruption of IT service and must be fixed and restored as soon as possible
	Maintenance	Scheduled maintenance must be performed to keep applications and infrastructure operating efficiently
	Keep the Lights On and Legal/Regulatory	The costs and resources required to support the basic steady state operations of the business, including some components of infrastructure
Discretionary* (Require ROI)	Major New/Change (Complex) Initiatives (Full Risk Mitigation)	Complex new initiatives or major changes (major enhancements or modifications) to systems, processes or infrastructure that provide new or additional functionality or capacity
	Fast Track (New/Change) (Simple or Limited Scope)	Simple new initiatives and minor changes that do not required the rigor and discipline of a complex initiative and be fast tracked.
	Standard (Repetitive) Request	Describe product/ service (functions, features and price in a product/service catalogue)
Strategic	Major initiative – Realistic ROI may not be doable – too early	A strategic initiative may fall into several categories – first market mover (new product or service); R & D; competitive advantage, etc.

* Note: Criteria for differentiating between complex or fast track initiatives or service catalogue listings will vary for each organization.

Figure 1.4 IT demand management classifications

Business/IT governance performance management and the Balanced Scorecard

A performance management plan must be developed for IT. The development of the performance management plan should be a collaborative effort between the business and IT. It should be based on a number of objectives, such as strategic, financials, customer, quality, process innovation, operational and service effectiveness which, in turn, support an organization's business vision, mission, plans, objectives and financials.

It is important to measure the performance of IT in terms that can be understood by the business. It is equally important to have two types of

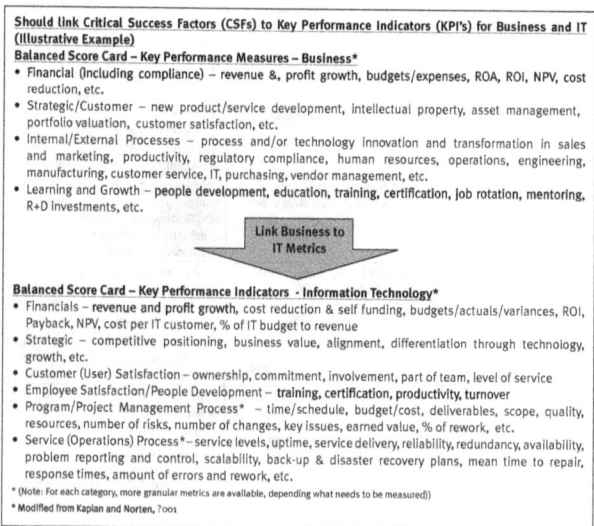

Should link Critical Success Factors (CSFs) to Key Performance Indicators (KPI's) for Business and IT (Illustrative Example)

Balanced Score Card – Key Performance Measures – Business*

- Financial (including compliance) – revenue &, profit growth, budgets/expenses, ROA, ROI, NPV, cost reduction, etc.
- Strategic/Customer – new product/service development, intellectual property, asset management, portfolio valuation, customer satisfaction, etc.
- Internal/External Processes – process and/or technology innovation and transformation in sales and marketing, productivity, regulatory compliance, human resources, operations, engineering, manufacturing, customer service, IT, purchasing, vendor management, etc.
- Learning and Growth – people development, education, training, certification, job rotation, mentoring, R+D investments, etc.

Link Business to IT Metrics

Balanced Score Card – Key Performance Indicators - Information Technology*

- Financials – revenue and profit growth, cost reduction & self funding, budgets/actuals/variances, ROI, Payback, NPV, cost per IT customer, % of IT budget to revenue
- Strategic – competitive positioning, business value, alignment, differentiation through technology, growth, etc.
- Customer (User) Satisfaction – ownership, commitment, involvement, part of team, level of service
- Employee Satisfaction/People Development – training, certification, productivity, turnover
- Program/Project Management Process* – time/schedule, budget/cost, deliverables, scope, quality, resources, number of risks, number of changes, key issues, earned value, % of rework, etc.
- Service (Operations) Process* – service levels, uptime, service delivery, reliability, redundancy, availability, problem reporting and control, scalability, back-up & disaster recovery plans, mean time to repair, response times, amount of errors and rework, etc.

* (Note: For each category, more granular metrics are available, depending what needs to be measured))

* Modified from Kaplan and Norten, ?oo1

Figure 1.5 Select Balanced Scorecard metrics for business and IT governance

reporting systems based on critical success factors and key performance indicators: those that are developed by IT for the external (out of IT) environment, such as executive management, the Board and the business managers, and those developed for internal use by IT management.

The execution of these plans and objectives must be monitored and measured by a combination of Balanced Scorecard key performance indicators (KPIs), as well as formal and informal status review meetings and reports (eg report cards, dashboards). Figure 1.6 illustrates high level business and IT Balanced Scorecard categories and related metrics. The outcomes should link critical success factors to KPIs that are measurable, part of a standard reporting system and linked to a governance component. If one cannot measure the result, they do not count. Chapter 8 provides more details on performance management, controls, Balanced Scorecard and other metrics.

1.3   Steps in making IT governance real

IT governance represents a journey towards continuous improvement and greater effectiveness. The journey is difficult, but can be facilitated by the following steps:

- must have a corporate mandate from the top - the Board and the executive team (including the CIO) committed to implementing and sustaining a robust governance environment
- must have dedicated and available resources - identify executive champion and multi-disciplinary team (to focus on each IT governance component)
- do homework – educate yourself on past, current and emerging best practices
- market the IT governance value propositions and benefits to the

organization - develop and conduct a communications, awareness and public relations campaign

- develop a tailored IT governance framework and roadmap for your organization based on current and emerging industry best practices
- assess the 'current state' of the level of IT governance maturity, or other frameworks that relate to specific IT governance components, such as project management maturity model (PMMM), vendor management (eSCM), performance management (Balanced Scorecard) and others, as a reference base (where are we today?), using a leading industry best practice framework such as CMMI or another framework that may apply to a specific component of IT governance
- develop a 'future state' IT governance blueprint (where you want to be) and keep it in focus
- decompose the IT governance components into well defined work packages (assign an owner and champion to each process component)
- develop an IT governance action plan, identify deliverables, establish priorities, milestones, allocate resources and measure progress
- sponsor organizational and individual certifications in the IT governance component areas, where they are available (eg PMP, ITIL, IT Security, IT Audit, BCP, Outsourcing, eSCM, COP, etc.)
- identify enabling technologies to support the IT governance initiative
- establish a 'web portal' to access IT governance policies, processes, information, communications and provide support
- market and communicate the IT 'value proposition' and celebrate wins
- plan for and sustain IT governance process improvements and link to a reward and incentive structure; create a 'continuous IT governance improvement' group to sustain the framework
- do not focus on specific ROI as a measure of success - use TCO (Total Cost of Operations) and business innovation and transformation metrics as measures of improvement

Avoiding IT governance implementation pitfalls

To avoid IT governance implementation pitfalls, key factors to remember
include the following:

- treat the implementation initiative as program or project with a series of
  phases with timetables and deliverables
- remember that implementation requires cultural change and
  transformation, which requires:
  - marketing of the value proposition and overcoming resistance to
    change
  - managing culture change and transformation
  - obtaining executive management buy-in and ownership
  - mobilizing commitment for change at multiple organization levels
- manage expectations of all constituents – IT governance takes time and
  represents a series of continuous improvement processes
- demonstrate measurable and incremental improvements in the
  environment and communicate them to the constituents

IT governance - current and future state transformation roadmap

In order to develop and/or improve the IT governance process, an
organization must assess its current and future governance state and
develop a transition roadmap for its IT transformation.

Figure 1.7 illustrates a roadmap for an organization to follow, as IT
transitions from its current state to its desired future state or environment.

IT Governance Process Improvement Flow - In order to develop and/or improve a governance process (business or IT), an organization must assess its current & future IT governance state and develop a plan to transform IT.

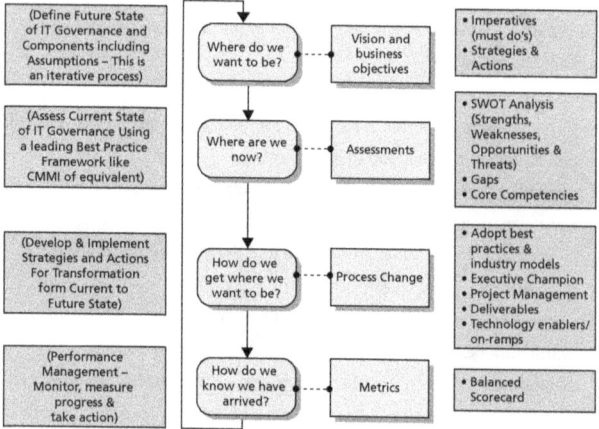

Figure 1.6 IT governance – current and future state transformation flow

Future state of IT governance – a blueprint concept

When all is said and done, most organizations would like to have an effective IT governance process and environment. Figure 1.8 identifies a blueprint of the 'ideal' future state and the key components that are necessary for effective governance deployment and strategic planning (business/IT alignment driven), application and infrastructure development (metrics driven) programs and projects and IT service support and delivery (metrics driven). Other components that should be added include architecture, security, business continuity, back-up and disaster recovery and related areas.

Strategic Planning (Business/IT Alignment Driven)

- Business and IT Leads are defined for each of an enterprise's core business process area
- The Business and IT Leads for each core business process jointly develop and prioritize requirements, and agree on a strategic alignment and investment plan
- The IT Leads also serve as the Single Point of Contact to their respective Business Unit Leads, address requests for new/changing requirements and address all service issues

SBU Requirements

Functional/Corporate Needs

(Finance)

Business Intelligence

Business/IT Exec. Steering Council

- Each core business process area submits its strategic roadmap together with business justification for review and approval, and finalizes them based on decisions made by the Business/IT Exec. Steering Council

- Business/IT Exec. Steering Council council sets top-down IT spending targets and allocation across business portfolios, reviews all strategic roadmaps and investment plans, prioritizes IT opportunities across all areas, defines key programs, approves final roadmaps and conducts periodic program/operating reviews

Application/Infrastructure Development (Metric Driven)/Programs/Projects

- IT establishes a Program Manager and budget for each key program approved by the Exec. Steering Council
- Each Program Manager initiates projects as specified on the approved roadmap by forming cross-functional Project Teams
- Project Teams receive formal authorization from PMO before initiating and closing projects, and releasing to production

Project 1 – New Initiative

Project Team

Project Team

Project 2 – Enhancement or Maintenance

Project Team

Project Team

- The Business and IT Leads complete more detailed business cases for programs in the roadmap

- PMO tracks the status of each active project, helps resolve issues and escalates critical issues to a PMO Steering Committee via a dashboard, and authorizes change management activities

Program Management Office (PMO)

Infrastructure Programs

Project Team

Project Team

- Internal or outsourced resources manage each technology domain

Service Support (Metric Driven)

User Support

- Internal or outsourced

Change/Risk Management

- Internal resources plan and manages change/risks using ITIL-compliant processes

Service Delivery (Metric Driven)

Planning & Implementation

- Internal resources plan and deliver services using ITIL-compliant processes

Infrastructure Operations

- Each Project Team executes its project by following well defined, repeatable methodologies/processes, and technical architecture standards
- Each Project Team draws its key resources from common pools of internal, Centers of Excellence, but outsources where appropriate

User Groups

Customers

Suppliers

Employees

SLA's KPIs

OLA's KPIs

Compliance

- All processes are documented and monitored for compliance

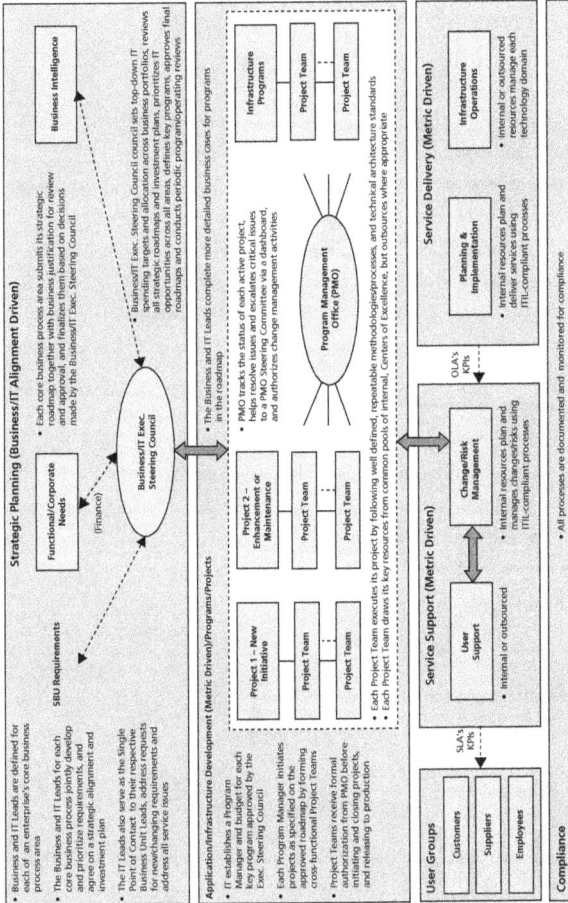

Figure 1.7 Future state IT governance: a blueprint concept

1.4   Summary and key take aways

Summary

IT governance is a broad and complex topic with many parts. IT governance represents a journey. It is not a one time event, and to achieve higher levels of IT maturity, IT governance should be persistently and relentlessly pursued, both from a top-down and a bottom-up perspective. Creating and sustaining a more effective IT governance environment will take time and resources, and should be focused on achieving incremental IT governance successes in priority areas, based on their value proposition or reduction of major 'pain point' to the organization.

It is critical to break down or segment the IT governance initiative into manageable, assignable and measurable components or work packages, with targeted deliverables. It is important to define clear roles for the Board, executive management and the IT governance project team, including ownership and accountability for each component and the overall initiative.

IT governance requires all three critical pillars to succeed: leadership, organization and people, scalable and flexible processes and enabling technologies.

Key take aways

The approach to IT governance must be consistent, but yet scalable, and tailored to each organization's environment and management style, key issues, opportunities, level of maturity, audit/legal requirements, available resources and cultural readiness. Remember, IT governance represents a journey, hopefully, towards higher levels of IT maturity, effectiveness and integration with the business.

Chapter 2
Overview of comprehensive IT governance framework and related industry best practice frameworks

2.1   Overview

There are a growing number of models and frameworks that address one or more aspects of IT governance. There are few that integrate the components necessary to plan, develop and deploy a comprehensive IT governance framework and roadmap to help guide organizational process improvement initiatives in this area.

- Some organizations use the COBIT® 4.0 (Control Objectives for Information and Related Technologies - IT Governance Institute, 2006) as a checklist focused primarily on the control aspects of improving IT governance.
- Others approach the problem from a security perspective and use ISO 17799 or BS 7799 as a framework.
- Meanwhile, others approach it from a project management perspective and use PMBOK® (Project Management Book of Knowledge - Project Management Institute, 2004) or PMMM® (Project Management Maturity Model – Crawford, 2002) or PRINCE2 (OGC, 1998).
- Others have embraced the IT Service Management model based on the ITIL® framework (IT Infrastructure Library – OGC, 2002).
- Several organizations have embarked on the quality improvement route through the use of ISO 9001-2000 or Six Sigma or Lean.

- Some use frameworks such as CMMI® (Capabilities Maturity Model Integrated – Software Engineering Institute, 2002, 2006) for systems and software development and eSCM® (eSourcing Capability Model developed for Service Providers and Customers to facilitate the outsourcing process by the ITSqc (IT Services Qualification Center at Carnegie Mellon University – Hyder, 2006; Hefley, 2006)).
- The University of Amsterdam developed a generic framework for information management which is being used in Europe (Akker, 1997).
- Efforts are being made by several groups to correlate CobiT with ITIL, ISO 17799, CMMI, PRINCE2, PMBOK, eSCM, ISO 9001, ISO 27001-2005 ISMS (Information Security Management Systems), AS 8000 and 8015, and other frameworks, and to streamline the use and application of these frameworks to improve the IT governance environment.

To establish and successfully deploy an IT governance initiative effectively, it must permeate the enterprise, and can be characterized as a mix of formal systematic processes blended with behavioral science techniques and people skills.

2.2 Integrated IT governance framework and roadmap

Many organizations start or focus the IT governance initiative on their highest 'pain' points or problem areas and expand from there. Given that most organizations are at different levels of maturity for each of the major components of IT governance or IT governance as a whole, there appears to be no single, best approach for all organizations. Rather, each organization should tailor its approach to its environment, and consider such factors as the organization's operating and management philosophy, key issues and opportunities, its change tolerance, state of level of maturity, audit and legal compliance requirements and its cultural readiness.

Whatever the variables, every organization must address each of the major components of IT governance including:

- **business strategy, plan and objectives (demand management)** - This involves the development of the business strategy and plan and this should drive the IT strategy and plan.
- **IT strategy, plan and objectives (demand management)** – This should be based on the business plan and objectives and should provide the direction and investment priorities of the IT functions and resources. This should also include portfolio investment management priorities, enterprise architecture and identify the decision rights (who influences decisions on IT and who is authorized to make the decisions on a wide variety of areas).
- **IT plan and service execution (execution management)** – This encompasses the processes required to assist in the execution of systems and services, such as program and project management, IT Service Management (including ITIL – IT Infrastructure Library), risk management, change management, security management, business and IT continuity, contingency, disaster recovery management and others.
- **performance management, management controls and compliance (execution management)** – This would include such areas as the Balanced Scorecard, key performance indicators, CobiT and regulatory compliance areas, management controls and audits including Sarbanes - Oxley, HIPPA, BASEL II and other general or industry specific regulations.
- **vendor management and outsourcing management (execution management)** – Since organizations are increasing their outsourcing spending as a percent of their budget, selecting and managing the service providers effectively has become more critical.
- **people development, continuous IT governance process improvement and learning** – To stay at the top of one's game, it has

also become critical to invest in learning and education, knowledge
management and continuous process improvement.

Most of today's IT models, frameworks and standards only address one
or a limited number of components that must be an integral part of a
comprehensive IT governance framework. Many of the current models are
being used by industry and should be understood, leveraged, integrated
and/or tailored. These should be used to develop an integrated approach
to IT governance. The proposed integrated IT governance framework
described in this chapter references the previously cited industry
frameworks, standards and guidelines, as well as additional ones that
are relevant for improving IT governance maturity and effectiveness in
organizations.

Figure 2.1 provides an illustration of the integrated IT governance
framework and its proposed major components, listing select references as
a pragmatic approach to improving the IT governance environment.

Figure 2.2 Illustrates a self-assessment model to assist companies to
determine their level of IT governance motivating by major component
and sub-component

2.3 Summary, implications and key take aways

Summary and implications

The growing number of current and emerging best practice frameworks,
guidelines and/or standards covering some aspects of IT governance, imply
that there is still no one, single, best way for all organizations to improve
the effectiveness and efficiency of their IT assets.

Identifies the major areas that must be addressed on the journey to a higher level of IT governance maturity and effectiveness

Areas of Work	Description/Components	Deliverables/References
Business Plan/ Objectives (Demand Management & Alignment)	• Strategic Business Plan – Vision, Objectives, Financials, Operations, SWOT, Imperatives (Must Do's), Initiatives (Alternatives that Support Imperatives), etc. • Capital Planning/Expense Planning & Budgeting • Business Performance Management (Key Metrics) • Executive and Other Steering & Review Councils; Organization Structure	• Plan Document • Financials • Balanced Scorecard Metrics • BCG; Porter; Hamel
IT Plan, Objectives, Portfolio Investment and Approvals (Demand Management & Alignment)	• IT Plan is aligned with the Business Plan – IT Capital/Expense Budget • IT portfolio investment, rationalization, selection, prioritization, funding and approval (Portfolio Management Model (for New, Change Programs and Projects and/or Operational and Infrastructure Functions) • Fund major initiatives • IT Performance Management (Define Metrics and Measurement Criteria)	• IT Strategic/Tactical Plan/ Metrics • Portfolio Mgt. Model (Investment Criteria); ITIM • Engagement Model - Roles • Business Rules & Authorization • McFarlan, Cash; Luftman; Popper; Selig
IT Plan Execution & Delivery (Resource & Execution Management)	• Program, Project and Operating Plans (Capital Plans, Project Plans and Budgets) • Policies, Standards, Guidelines & Processes (e.g. Management Control, Enterprise Architecture, Security, PMO, ITIL, Enterprise Architecture, etc.) • Processes (PMO, Help Desk, Security, Administrative SOPs, Workflows, Change, Risk, etc.) • Financial, program, project, application, maintenance and operational accountability	• Assess Implications of PMMM, PMBOK, CMMI, ITIL, SDLC, CoBit, Security (ISO 17799), Prince2 ,eSCM Frameworks • Infrastructure & Operational Integrity, Continuity & Security
Performance Management, Controls, Risk, Compliance and Vendor Management (Execution Management)	• Manage and measure plans, budgets programs, projects, operations & risks • Define and track key performance indicators (KPI) • Compare plans to actuals and take appropriate corrective actions • Outsourcing and Vendor Selection, Tracking, Measurement • Business and IT Continuity, Security, Contingency and Disaster Recovery	• Balanced Scorecard & KPIs • Performance Management • RFI, RFQ, RFP and Contract Management; • Sarbanes-Oxley ++ Compliance • Management Controls/ COBIT
People Development, Continuous Process Improvement & Learning	• Human capital development • Organizational, Project & Operational Maturity Models and Standards • Managing Change and Transformation (e.g. culture, interoperability) • Training and Certification (e.g. Individual and Organization)	• Adopt Current and Emerging Industry and Government Best Practices Standards & Guidelines • PCMM; OMB 300; ISO; ITIM • Career Development and Certification

Figure 2.1 Integrated IT governance framework

- There are a growing number of continuous improvement frameworks and models that apply to IT governance and one or more of its major components.
- All of them focus on helping either individuals and/or organizations improve their effectiveness, competencies and maturity levels in one or more areas of IT governance.
- Most of the current practices do not provide the details of 'how to do' IT governance from a strategic top-down and pragmatic bottom-up perspective.
- An organization should leverage, adopt and tailor those models, frameworks and/or standards that address those issues, opportunities,

The template can be used to assess the level of IT Governance and its major components, process, maturity and effectiveness (1=low; 5=high). Additional IT Governance components from COBIT, ISO 17799 or others may be added across the horizontal axis as required.

Maturity	Attributes	Demand Management and Alignment (Chapter 3)				Execution Management (Chapters 5,6,7)							Performance Management and Controls (Chapter 8)					People Development and Learning (Chapter 4)			
		Business Plan	IT Plan	Portfolio Investment Management	Other	Program/Project Management	Resource Management	Risk Management	ITSM + ITIL	Vendor Management	Enterprise Architecture	Other	Critical Success Factors/CSFs	Key Performance Indicators	MBO's and incentives tied to CSFs	Controls and Audit (COBIT)	Other	Continuous Process Improvement	Knowledge Management	Education, Training and Learning	Other
Level 5	• Optimized proces																				
Level 5	• Metrics driven process improvements																				
Level 4	• Process managed and used by all																				
Level 3	• Enterprise wide process and standards																				
Level 2	• Basic Process																				
Level 2	• Basic Knowledge																				
Level 1	• Ad hoc																				
Level 1	• No established practices or processes																				
	Major IT Governance Components)	Values																			

Figure 2.2 IT governance maturity – a self assessment model

pain points and threats most critical to the organization and create an IT governance roadmap with clearly defined the roles and responsibilities for IT governance development, process ownership and continuous improvement.

Figure 2.3 provides a summary of the key frameworks that enable IT governance continuous improvement, their general use and sources.

MODEL	GENERAL USE	SOURCE(S)
COBIT®	IT Control Objectives	ITGI (IT Governance Institute)
ITIM	IT Investment Management	GSA (General Services Administration)
Kano	Customer Needs and Requirements	Kano
CMMI®	Systems and Software Development and Systems Integration	SEI (Software Engineering Institute)
Balanced Scorecard	Corporation Measurement Scheme	Kaplan and Norton
e-Sourcing Capability Model	Sourcing (for both Service Providers and Customers)	ITsqc (IT Services Qualification Center)
People - CMM® (P-CMM)	Human Asset Management	SEI
ISO® 9001:2000	Quality Management	ISO (International Standards Organizations)
Six Sigma®	Quality Management and Process Improvement	Motorola
ISO® / IEC 17799 and 27001	Information Security Management	ISO
ISO® 20000/ BS 15000 / ITIL®	IT Infrastructure, Service and Operations Management	ISO / British Standards Organization / ITSMF (IT Service Management Forum)
PMBOK® / OPM3® / PMMM / PRINCE2®	Program and Project Management	PMI (Project Management Institute) / Project Management Solutions, Inc./ CCTA (OGC – Office of Government Commerce)
OPBOK®	Outsourcing	IAOP (International Association of Outsourcing Professionals)
Generic Framework for IT Management	IT Management	University of Amsterdam and Henderson and Venkatraman

CMMI® and People–CMMI® are registered trademarks of Carnegie Mellon University. COBIT® is a registered trademark of the IT Governance Institute (ITGI). ISO® is a registered trademark of the International Organization for Standardization. ITIL® is a registered trademark of the U.K. Office of Government Commerce. Six Sigma® is a trademark of Motorola, Inc.

Figure 2.3 Summary of current and emerging frameworks that enable IT governance and continuous improvement.

Other titles published by Van Haren Publishing cover frameworks in more detail.

Key take aways

The selection of a particular framework or combination of frameworks is largely dependent on the strategic objectives, available resources of an organization and their desired outcomes. All of the frameworks require the management of change and cultural transformation.

The IT governance framework model provides a comprehensive framework, based on a key set of required components that should provide an appropriate baseline to develop a roadmap to steer a more effective journey towards a higher level of IT maturity for organization. However, each organization must tailor its approach to address its environment, current level of maturity, pain points and other factors.

Chapter 3
Business and IT alignment, strategic/operating planning and portfolio investment management excellence (demand management)

3.1 Overview

As business and technology have become increasingly intertwined, the strategic alignment of the two has emerged as a major corporate issue. Co-operation and collaboration is becoming increasingly important in the modern business environment. The resulting emergence of new forms of relationships is challenging managers to understand fundamental dynamics of co-operation, in order to evaluate and restructure their relationships.

Alignment focuses on activities that IT and business executives within an organization should do, to work together to meet the business goals and to make the organization more effective. "CIO's who achieve alignment typically do so by establishing a set of well-planned process improvement programs that systematically address obstacles and go beyond executive level conversation to permeate the entire IT organization and its culture" (Clemons, Rowe and Redi, 1992).

Successful business/IT alignment means developing and sustaining relationship between IT and business that benefits both parties. This requires that IT executives be recognized as essential to the development of credible business strategies and operations, and business executives be considered equally essential to the development of credible IT strategies and operations.

Key questions to address in improving business and IT alignment include:

- How can organizations align their businesses more effectively?
- How can organizations assess and measure alignment?
- How can organizations improve their alignment?
- How can organizations achieve higher levels of alignment maturity?
- Do your processes and related measurements recognize and take into account the strong co-dependencies between the business and IT people, processes and technology?
- What information is critical to support the strategic business plan initiatives and objectives?
- What changes in business direction (and priorities) are planned or anticipated for the plan period?
- What are the current/projected major business/functional opportunities, issues, risks, threats and constraints?
- What strategic or tactical value does IT provide to your business or function?
- How can IT add more strategic value to the business (eg revenue growth; cost reduction/containment/avoidance, reduce speed to market, business process transformation, business/competitive intelligence, etc.)?
- Is IT developing and maintaining superior and constructive relationships with customers, vendors and others? How can they be improved?
- How effectively is IT communicating its progress and problems to its constituents? Is a relationship and engagement model used?
- What governance processes and controls have been instituted in IT?
- Does the Board/operating committee/senior business leadership review and approve the IT strategy, priorities and funding?

Forrester Research developed a template for helping organizations to assess the level of IT and business alignment maturity. Figure 3.1 represents the alignment maturity assessment model that can be used by organizations to assess where they are today, and also as a base line to develop a plan for achieving a higher level of alignment maturity in the future.

Level	Phase	Description
5	Optimized Process	There is advanced understanding of IT and business strategy alignment. **Processes have been refined to a level of external best practices, based** on results of continuous improvement and maturity modeling with other organizations. External experts are leveraged, and benchmarks are used for guidance. Monitoring, self-assessment, and communication about alignment expectations are pervasive.
4	Defined and Managed Process	The need for IT and business strategy alignment is understood and accepted. **A baseline set of processes is defined, documented, and** integrated into strategic and operational planning. Measurement criteria are developed, and activity is monitored. Overall accountability is clear, and management is rewarded based on results.
3	Repeatable Processes	There is awareness of alignment issues across the enterprise. Alignment activities are under development, which include processes, structures, and educational activities. Some strategy alignment takes place in some business units but not across the entire enterprise. Some attempts are made to measure and quantify the benefits.
2	Initial Processes	There is evidence that the organization recognizes the need to align IT and business strategy. However, there are no standard processes. There are fragmented attempts, often on a case-by-case basis within individual business units.
1	Ad hoc	There is a complete lack of any effort to align IT and business strategy. IT functions in a purely support role.

Source: Modified from Forrester Research, Inc.

Figure 3.1 IT/Business Alignment Maturity Assessment Template

The role of the Board and executive management

The Board and executive management must play an increasingly important role in facilitating the alignment of the business and IT. This should include the following activities:

- Assess that the IT strategy and plan are aligned with the organization's strategy and plan.

- Evaluate whether IT is delivering against the strategy through clear objectives, expectations and key performance indicators (KPIs).
- Direct IT strategy by determining the level of IT investments, balancing the investments between growing the enterprise and supporting the on-going operations of the enterprise.
- Ensure an open and collaborative culture between IT and the business.

The changing role of the CIO

In the past, many organizations have practiced a reactive approach to IT, by defining the CIO's priorities by what had to be done – taking cost out, ensuring the continuity of the business, maintaining the integrity, security and privacy of data, etc., as well as keeping pace with the changing demands of the business.

Today a number of world class enterprises have recognized the enormous impact that IT can make – not only on growth and responsiveness, but also on innovation and business transformation. In these organizations, IT is a business enabler. These organizations recognize that information technology can provide business leverage and be a driver of top-line growth. They look to their CIO for the ability to drive this growth. They are using technology to increase efficiency across the business and to enable the business to integrate and exploit new requirements more easily. They are also using technology to provide new distribution channels, understand different ways to segment markets and develop profound new customer and market insights. Superior alignment of the business with IT represents a key success factor and represents a 'win-win' environment for both the business and IT.

Components of effective alignment

According to Luftman, Papp and Brier, *"Achieving alignment is evolutionary and dynamic. It requires strong support from senior management, good working relationships, strong leadership, appropriate prioritization, trust, and effective communications, as well as thorough understanding of the business environment"* (Luftman, Papp and Brier, 1999).

Henderson and Venkatraman first developed a strategic alignment model in 1990 which was modified by Luftman, Papp and Brier in 1999, based on a study of over 500 firms representing 15 industries. The model consists of twelve components and it is the relationship and the processes linking each of the components that define business-IT alignment (Henderson and Venkatraman, 1990; Luftman, Papp and Brier, 1999).

The components of the model, which have been further modified by the author, are:

Business strategy:
- **business scope** – includes the industry, markets, products, services, customers, regulations and locations where an enterprise competes as well as the competitors, suppliers and other constituents that affect the competitive business environment
- **distinctive competencies** – the critical success factors and core competencies that provide a firm with a potential competitive edge; this includes brand and marketing, research and development, manufacturing and/or operations and new product development, innovation (eg product, process and/or technology), cost and pricing structure, and sales and distribution channels, logistics and supply chain management and culture
- **business governance** – this involves companies establishing the relationship amongst management, stockholders and the board

of directors; also included is how the companies are affected by government regulations, and how the firm manages its relationships and alliances with strategic partners; finally, the performance management, measurements and controls.

Organization processes and infrastructure:

- **administration structure** – the way the firm organizes and structures its business and defines the decision rights, authority and accountability; examples include centralized, decentralized, matrix, horizontal, vertical, geographic, federal, and functional organizations
- **processes** - how the firm's business activities (the work performed by employees) operate or flow; major issues include value added activities, process improvement and integration and interface points between functions, departments or business units and external forces
- **skills** – people considerations such as how to hire/fire, motivate, train/ educate, incentivize, manage change and culture

IT strategy:

- **technology scope** - the important information applications, data management and technologies
- **systematic competencies** - those capabilities (eg access to information that is important to the creation/achievement of a company's strategies) that distinguish the IT services
- **IT governance** - how the authority for resources, risk, and responsibility for IT is shared between business partners, IT management and service providers; program and project selection, prioritization and approval issues are included here

IT processes and infrastructure

- **architecture** -the technology priorities, policies, and choices that allow applications, software, networks, hardware, and data management to be integrated into a cohesive platform

- **processes** - those practices and activities carried out to develop synergistic plans with business, develop and maintain applications, manage IT infrastructure and institutionalize consistent IT governance processes
- **skills** - IT human resource considerations such as how to hire/fire, motivate, train/educate, incentivize, change and culture

Enablers of business/IT alignment

According to a study by IBM's Advanced Business Institute, the key enablers to business and IT alignment include: (IBM, 1999)
- senior executive support for IT
- IT involved in business strategy development
- IT understands the business
- business – IT partnership
- well-prioritized IT projects
- IT demonstrates leadership

Both the IT and business executives and professionals should co-operate to build up a comprehensive strategy that will lead to formulating a process of continuous improvement for more effective alignment. For example, one firm that successfully used cross-functional teams for strategy development includes Bristol-Myers Squibb. At Bristol-Myers Squibb, an IT Review Board composed of IT and business executives lead the strategy and planning processes, identify opportunities, and defines priorities for IT. It also tracks projects and uses the concept of an IT–business liaison to maintain and ensure closer collaboration.

Inhibitors of business/IT alignment

The alignment inhibitors are:
- IT and the business lack close relationships and may not have common goals

- IT does not prioritize projects well and in a timely manner
- IT fails to meet its commitments
- IT does not understand the core business or mission of the organization
- senior executives do not understand the value of IT, and therefore are not committed
- IT management lacks dynamic business-oriented leadership

The inhibitors of alignment are the reverse of the enablers. The first inhibitor is the lack of a close relationship between the business and the IT function. In some organizations, IT executives do not participate in any strategy formulation meetings, nor have a seat at the 'C' suite. One other indicator is where the CIO reports to the CFO. This represents a constraint and handicap to more effective alignment. If these initiatives are not well defined and prioritized, then the IT department could be spending time and resources on projects that are not important to the business. Only business executives (as sponsors or champions or owners) can drive and validate the realization of value from IT related projects. It is critical to have a strong partnership to ensure better collaboration and bonding. The vehicles for this governance process include collaborative steering committees, IT and business liaisons, budget and human resource allocation processes, value assessments and a seat for the IT executive at the executive ('C') table.

Select alignment metrics

The business and IT department need to collaborate and develop accurate metrics that are linked to the business objectives, priorities and performance. Listed below are some examples of alignment metrics:

- revenue growth
- return on investment
- decrease in total cost of ownership (TCO)

- increase in employee productivity
- business process cost and time reduction
- speed to market
- customer satisfaction
- increase quality of products and services
- number of IT and business strategic planning and operational review meetings
- development and use of a business and IT engagement and relationship partnership model

Business and IT alignment and demand management

Demands for IT services are either planned or unplanned, and generally come in several flavors – mandatory or core ('must do's' such as service interruptions, standard maintenance, keeping the lights on and/or regulatory compliance) and discretionary ('could do's' if aligned, feasible, cost justified and/or strategic). In an ideal world, both mandatory and discretionary requests should be approved by the business/IT leadership if they have been identified in the IT strategic and operating plans, in accordance with the organization's decision rights and approval authority guidelines. The following considerations will further help align business needs with IT:

- Clearly define the value (eg cost reduction, containment and avoidance; increased revenues; faster access to information; shorter time to market etc.) that IT provides in support of the business. Identify value adding activities (eg value chain and other business models/attributes) and strategies that would enhance them through IT.
- Focus on listening to the voice of the customer and develop a business/ IT engagement and relationship building model.
- Ensure that all IT initiatives are evaluated using a consistent, but flexible set of investment selection, prioritization and approval criteria

to assure a strong link to the business plan, deployment and integrated into the on-going operations. (See Figure 3.2 – IT/business alignment, portfolio investment management and project management triangle). The figure identifies key selection criteria such as new/incremental revenues, strategic fit, ROI, intellectual capital, cost reduction, business transformation and other criteria and once approved, shows the project management and life cycle components before the initiative is implemented and operationalized.

- Develop a strategic IT plan that identifies major initiatives, technical/ architecture, operational, organizational, people development and financial objectives and measurements in support of the business.

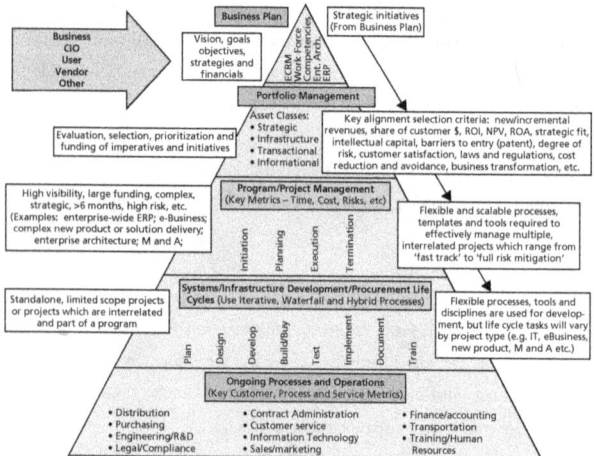

Figure 3.2 IT/business alignment, project selection and portfolio investment management triangle

Figure 3.3 illustrates an example of IT investment spend alternatives and the percent of investments in each category for a technology organization. These should be driven by business needs and priorities, and will vary by organization and from year to year, based on the organization's business strategy and objectives. It is interesting to note that for this particular organization, the projected spend is segmented into three major 'buckets' or investment portfolios:

- Portfolio 1 – revenue growth projects – focus IT projects on such areas as new product development, customer relationship management, customer interface systems, distribution systems, marketing and e-commerce and others.
- Portfolio 2 – cost reduction, avoidance and containment projects – focus on business transformation, innovation, quality, supply chain, ERP systems, etc.
- Portfolio 3 – business enablement projects – contain several areas such as infrastructure, service delivery, compliance, employee development and governance. Others can also be added.

Based on the business strategy and plan of an organization, the percent spend should change from year to year, and will also vary by organization and industry.

A global insurance company example of a world class IT alignment governance process

AXA Equitable is a New York-based, wholly owned subsidiary of the giant financial services firm AXA, which is headquartered in Paris. AXA Equitable has about 10,000 employees in the US, with about 500 in the IT organization. In 1999, AXA US decided to increase its investment in IT significantly. As a result, there was a proliferation of projects that seemed to be chosen based on qualitative analysis alone.

IT Investment Management Portfolio Alternatives Consist of Discretionary (Optional), Strategic and Mandatory (Keep the Lights On) Requirements and the Amount of Investment % in Each Portfolio Should be Driven by Business Needs and Will Change from Year to Year and Organization to Organization

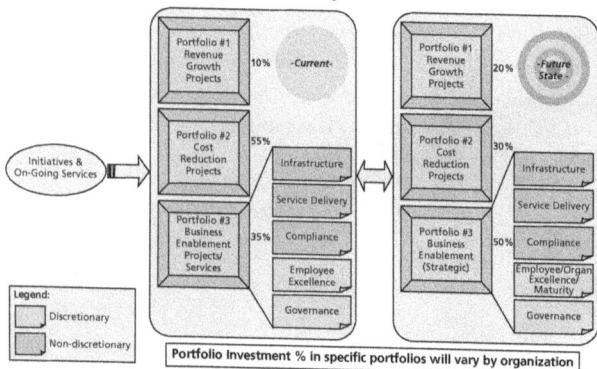

Figure 3.3 Strategic IT investment spend alternatives

Since alignment represented the front end of the IT governance framework and it was a 'big pain point' for the company that had to be corrected, the company's IT governance improvement initiative started there. The VP of AXA-Technology Services Strategic Management Office, was tasked with establishing a fair and accepted means of choosing among a large array of prospective IT investments – that is, develop a governance process – based on business analysis and a sound economic model that aligned IT investments much more objectively and closely, with the business.

The business and IT alignment and governance component was designed with the following elements:

- **Executive top-down governance direction** – A business/IT governance committee was formed consisting of the CEO and his direct reports, which included the CIO and business unit heads, to determine IT spend levels on IT initiatives for the company. Each initiative had to undergo two filters, one focused on the alignment of business objectives with IT initiatives first, and the second focused on cost/benefit analysis.

- **Filter 1 – Business and IT strategy alignment** – The first filter involved the identification and weighting of key business strategy objectives (eg increase revenue by 25%; reduce expense base by 30%; improve customer satisfaction by 15%, etc.) These objectives were plotted on an X-Y chart with corresponding IT projects, which were ranked by five levels of potential impact (eg extreme, strong, moderate, low and none). To help focus on the most important business objectives, all projects classified by the executive governance committee as having extreme, strong and medium impact on the business were identified in a 'Strategic Alignment Master List', which represented preliminary approval for further consideration and provided the input document for Filter 2. Concurrently, a 'total pool of money' was allocated for IT projects for the coming plan year, which was further segmented into two parts, the business-as-usual part (funds to keep the operation going and the lights on) and the discretionary portion (where the investment choices had to be made). In addition, separate 'buckets' of budget allocations were established for corporate and business unit projects.

- **Filter 2 – IT project business case** – For the top ranked projects identified in Filter 1, IT, with the business developed a business case to determine the costs and benefits (eg ROI, NPV, payback, risks, etc.). Based on a combination of Filter 1 and 2 ranking, a priority list of projects was developed. The 'pool of IT project money' was allocated to the priority project list until the funds were fully allocated. The remaining unfunded projects were postponed, recycled or cancelled.

- **PMO handoff** – Those projects that were approved at the executive governance committee meeting were assigned to the project management office for assignments to the appropriate department, for development and deployment through the project management life cycle process.

The case was published and summarized by Gartner. The results of the AXA IT investment governance process were very positive. There was a strong sense of direction and rationality regarding how the business is using IT to advance its position. The methodology has been applied outside of IT, but within other AXA organizations.

This model has been implemented as a continuous improvement process that links strategy, governance and budget. Enterprises must determine the strategic direction they want to take, decide on the best investments for maximizing progress in that direction, and then allocate the budget and time for implementation. As projects proceed and the environment changes, it is necessary to track and modify the program in a seamless fashion. In essence, the insurance company used a two-tier weighted scoring model to align IT projects more closely with the business, and it is working for them.

In summary, for IT investments to be aligned with the business more closely, they must be prioritized, both by their impact on helping the business to achieve its objectives, and by the result of a business case analysis. It is also critical that this 'approved master list of aligned projects' is allocated the right resources to complete the projects.

3.2 Principles of aligning IT to the business more effectively

Based on the research (including a review of best practice organizations such as GE, Sun, IBM, Starwood Hotels, Unilever, Avon, United Technologies and others), there are several strategic planning, management control and supplementary principles and practices, which when deployed well, will improve the business and IT alignment environment. They include, but are not limited to the following:

Strategic Planning Practices:
This should be a formal process developed as a partnership and contract (in the loose definition of the word) between the business and IT. It should clearly focus on defining and relating the value that IT provides in support of the business. Specific planning principles and practices should be deployed such as (Selig, 1983):

- **Strategic planning program and processes** - Develop a strategic IT plan that is an integral part of the strategic business plan. The plan framework, format and process should be consistent, repeatable and similar, allowing for functional differences between the business units, and between functions and IT, to facilitate alignment and integration.
- **Executive steering committee(s)** – This involves top management in the IT/ business planning process, to establish overall IT direction, investment levels and approval of major initiatives across the enterprise. Each business unit and corporate staff function should have an equivalent body, to focus on their respective areas, to establish priorities and formalize periodic reviews.
- **Investment portfolio management, capital and expense planning and budgeting** – This ensures that all IT investments are evaluated, prioritized, funded, approved and monitored, using a consistent, but flexible process, and a common set of evaluation criteria, that are linked to the strategic and annual operating plans and budgets, both capital and expense, at multiple organizational levels.
- **Performance management and measurement** – This monitors strategic plan outcomes based on specific Balanced Scorecard and service level measurement categories and metrics, and establishes organizational and functional accountability linked to MBO (management by objectives) performance criteria and reviews.
- **Planning guidelines and requisites** – A set of general instructions describing the format, content and timing of the business and IT plans; these are general in nature, as opposed to specific standards, and

should provide the business units with some latitude and flexibility to accommodate local conditions.

Management Control Practices:

These management control practices focus on the tactical and operating plans and programs, and on the day-to-day operational environment.

- **Formalize multi-level IT/business functional/operations/technology steering and governance boards** with specific roles and decision rights in the day-to-day implementation and Service Management of the tactical IT plans, programs and services.
- **Tactical/operating plans and resource allocation** establishes annual and short-term IT objectives, programs, projects and the resources to accomplish the objectives (eg application development plan, infrastructure refresh plan, etc.).
- **Budget/accounting/charge-back** establishes budgets, and monitors expenditures; charges IT costs back to the business or functional users to ensure more effective involvement and ownership by the business.
- **Performance management and measurement** collects, analyzes and reports on performance of results against objectives at a more detailed and operational level than at the strategic plan level (see Chapter 8 - Performance Management). In addition, formal periodic monthly and quarterly review meetings should be held to review the status of major initiatives and the on-going performance of IT.

Supplementary Practices:

These programs will vary by organization, and can result in improving alignment:

- **IT/customer engagement and relationship model** - establishes a customer-focused relationship model to facilitate interfaces, decisions, resolution of issues, collaborative plan development and better communications, and build trust between IT and the business.

- **Program management office (PMO)** – establishes the processes, tools and IT/business unit roles and responsibilities for program and project management. Initially, PMOs were established by IT to help manage IT programs and projects. As organizations recognize the increased benefits that a PMO brings to an environment, PMOs are being established at the executive level by a growing number of organizations, to ensure that major corporate business initiatives utilize the same discipline and structure as IT initiatives, to implement them within scope, on-time, within budget and to the customer's satisfaction.

- **Marketing, public relations and communications program for IT** – given that most IT departments are particularly poor at promoting and marketing their accomplishments and value, this function creates awareness and promotes executive, management and employee education and commitment, to the value of IT in support of the business, through newsletters, websites, press releases, testimonials and other marketing and public relation events.

- **IT charter** – promotes effective and definitive interaction and links between IT and the business/functional groups they support. A charter can provide information on scope, roles and responsibilities, and provide specific program or project authority and limit to that authority.

- **Standards and guidelines** – adopt and maintain best practice standards and flexible guidelines to describe and document IT alignment, investment and planning processes, policies and procedures for IT governance and other areas within IT. A financial services organization developed a simple guideline for its customers entitled, '*How to Request IT Services and Get Them Approved*', which was a major success.

- **Organizational and people development, skills and competencies** – develop a proactive learning environment by encouraging and rewarding education, training and certification (where appropriate).

- **Annual/semi-annual IT management meeting** – conduct regular IT/ business management meetings to share best practices, develop stronger relationships, and address organization-wide issues and opportunities.

3.3   Setting a direction for improved alignment through planning related processes

The strategic, annual and project plans of an organization must be aligned with to corresponding business. To ensure that the IT organization is focusing on the appropriate investments, and providing the level of service necessary in support of business operations and transformation, each significant IT objective must be linked to a specific business objective with a business owner, who is accountable for evaluating the performance towards that objective. In a large US manufacturing company, individual IT units submit lists of proposed projects and budgets. A corporate group assembles these lists and helps business executives evaluate and approve the investments. In a survey conducted by CIO Magazine, *'plan reviews and project prioritization was rated as the most effective practice to establish IT and business alignment'*. (CIO Magazine, May, 2004)

The importance of business and IT planning has been identified by many individual and corporate researchers over the years. Planning allows organisations to:
- identify and focus on critical issues, opportunities, objectives, scope and deliverables in a phased and structured manner
- minimize risks, obstacles and constraints
- provide a roadmap and process for action
- obtain a better understanding of the alternatives
- provide a baseline for monitoring and controlling work and progress
- establish a foundation for more effective communications, commitment, buy-in and consensus building
- better anticipation and planning for change
- better management of expectations of all constituents

Many businesses and IT planning processes and techniques have been documented in previous research, such as IBM's *Business Systems Planning*,

Richard Nolan's *Stages of Growth*, John Rockart's *Critical Success Factors*, John Porter's *Value Chain Analysis and Competitive Forces Model* and many others. Some of these are very complex and detailed, while others are more streamlined.

Key principles for effective business/IT strategic plan alignment

IT plans should be developed hand-in-hand with the business and updated as necessary. Additional principles that strengthen plan alignment include:

- **ownership** - CIO with involvement of IT leadership and of the executive officers and business unit leadership
- **frequency** – IT strategic plan is written/revised/refreshed annually, although major changes may cause the plan to be updated more frequently
- **time horizon** – IT strategic plan usually covers a three year period, with annual operating plans identifying capital and expense budget levels for the first year of the plan cycle
- **plan process** – IT reviews the business strategic plan major objectives, themes and priorities with the business units and corporate services
- **IT interviews** the business units - to align and map IT objectives, initiatives and priorities with the business, using the key plan questions and discussion topics
- **IT identifies** major new or enhancement business application or service support initiatives - as well as significant technology refresh requirements (eg replace obsolete technology; support anticipated growth and new infrastructure requirements).
- The **business-driven initiatives and the infrastructure initiatives** - are combined in the IT strategic plan (which includes a rough estimate of capital funding needs) and presented to the executive operating committee and SBU heads for approval

- **Communication of the IT strategic plan** – a short version (highlights) of the approved plan is posted on the IT web intranet and reviewed with the IT department and appropriate business constituents
- **Link to annual operating plan and budget plan** – the annual capital and expense budget are approved by the Executive Team for the initiatives identified in the plan; often, new or break-fix initiatives come up during the year (which are not in original plan) that require prioritization, funding and resources; a formal portfolio investment management approval process is followed for that purpose
- **Link to portfolio of projects for annual operating plan** – once the annual operating plan and budget have been approved, a project list and related business cases are prepared, prioritized and reviewed; projects charters are developed for approved projects, and the appropriate implementation resources are allocated and/or committed
- **Link to annual MBOs (management by objectives), performance measurements, KPIs and rewards/incentives** – both the strategic plan and annual operating plan must be driven by measurable outcomes (eg cost, time, profit, volume, customer satisfaction, strategic competitive value, etc.) and appropriate management actions taken according to positive or negative results

Another good example of a well publicized alignment turnaround case is Toyota Motor, USA. In 2002, the Toyota business units and IT were not aligned, and the IT organization lost their credibility with the business due to late projects, high costs, poor perceived business value and physical isolation of key IT liaison managers from the business.

Recognizing this fact, the CIO took the following steps to regain IT's credibility and improve its alignment with the business (Wailgum, April 15, 2005):

- **Established the Toyota Value Action Program** - A team of eight staff
  were established and responsible for translating the CIO's vision into
  actionable items. The team identified 18 business-driven initiatives,
  including increasing employee training and development, gaining cost
  savings, making process improvements, resolving inefficiencies and
  implementing a metrics program. Each initiative got a project owner
  and a team. The CIO insisted that each initiative have one or more
  metrics to check its success.
- **Established the office of the CIO** - This most significant initiative
  called for improved alignment with the business side. At the heart of this
  new effort would be a revamped 'office of the CIO' structure, with new
  roles, reporting lines and responsibilities for business and IT executives.
- **Implemented a business/IT engagement model** - As part of the
  overhaul, the CIO took top-flight personnel out of the IT building and
  embedded them as divisional information officers, or DIOs, in all of the
  business unit locations. These DIOs were accountable for IT strategy,
  development and services, and they sat on the management committees
  headed by top business executives. The DIOs' goal was to forge
  relationships with tier-one and tier-two execs (VP and senior director
  levels). *'I still believe in managing IT centrally, but it was incumbent on us
  to physically distribute IT into the businesses'*, commented the CIO. *'They
  could provide more local attention while keeping the enterprise vision alive'*.
  The difference between the previous relationship managers and the new
  DIOs was that DIOs have complete accountability and responsibility for
  the business area they serve, together with their business counterparts.
- **'Town hall' meeting** - Similarly, IT senior management held 'town hall'
  meetings to announce the changes and deal with questions.
- **Pay for performance** – For the first time, the CIO also tied part of
  the senior IT managers' bonuses to their success in meeting the goals
  of each of their annual plans. These managers are judged on 10 areas
  and on how well they meet the objectives in those areas; for example,
  meeting project-based goals (whether the project was done on time and

on budget) and operational goals (implementing new governance and portfolio management processes).

- **Executive steering committee** - To further strengthen the IT-business bond, the CIO chartered the executive steering committee, or ESC, to approve all major IT projects. The executive steering committee controls all of the project funds in one pool of cash, and it releases funds for each project as each phase of the project's goals are achieved. Everyone in the company can look at what money was (and was not) going to be spent. The pool's administrators can sweep unused funds out, and other projects can go after those funds.

The CIO said that the organizational structure today is *'almost unrecognizable'* to the IT employees she inherited. One key element of success was rotating IT people into other parts of the company and bringing business people into IT.

Business and IT strategy and plan development frameworks

As mentioned previously, a pragmatic business and IT planning process used successfully in industry is called 'pressure point analysis', and it can be used to develop both business and IT plans. It is primarily based on analyzing internal and external pressures and trends, and addressing six basic questions:

- **Where are we?** This question establishes the base line or current state reference base for either the business or IT plans. It considers internal factors, such the strengths, weaknesses, opportunities and threats. It also identifies core competencies and any gaps in the strategy. External trends and pressures such as industry, competition, globalization, life style, regulations, technology, economics and environmental factors are evaluated, as well as customer and prospect input.

- **Why change?** Since change is inevitable and rapid, these are the assumptions on which the current base line, plan and strategy will change. As Hamel stated, 'if organizations are to survive and prosper, they must continuously reinvent themselves' (Hamel, 2000). This question identifies the reasons and motivations for change, and examines high level alternatives for the business or IT to consider.

- **What could we do?** If there were no constraints based on an organization, this question helps them to contemplate what could be done'

- **What should we do?** This question narrows the strategic choices based on a company's vision, objectives and direction, and any constraints such as capital, people resources, time, intellectual property, existing knowledge and experience, and the risk of the initiative. It addresses the question of why that vision and its related goals, objectives and strategies are possible and what should be done.

- **How do we get there?** Any business or IT plan should have 'mandatory' strategies if an organization is to grow and prosper. These mandatory strategy classifications are called imperatives. For a business plan, select imperatives can include continual growth, maximizing customer intimacy, maximizing shareholder value, achieving operational excellence and integrating technology into the organization seamlessly. How this is done will vary by organization, and Figure 3.4 suggests some choices.

From the IT point of view, the imperatives can include such factors as enterprise and information architecture, maximizing customer intimacy, new applications in support of the business, effective IT service and infrastructure management and finally, people and process development and improvement. For each business or IT imperatives, multiple actions can be pursued. Examples of select alternative strategies are provided in Figure 3.5 and Figure 3.6, which illustrate the business and IT strategy and plan development frameworks respectively.

- **Did we get there?** This question deals with performance metrics and management controls to ensure that the plan goals and objectives are met.

IT plan outlines

IT plan outlines and contents vary widely from company to company. However, to put a stake in the ground, a generic business plan outline for a generic company is outlined in Figure 3.6. By applying the six questions previously described to the outline, a plan can be generated.

Business and IT strategic planning cycle and alignment

The IT planning cycle should closely parallels the business planning cycle. IT plans should be developed iteratively with the business.

Figure 3.7 illustrates a manufacturing company's strategic planning process and timetable. It identifies the roles of the business and IT leaders, starting in the first quarter of the plan year and culminating in approved projects and initiatives in the last quarter of the plan year, which becomes the tactical or operating master project plan for the following year.

Can be used as a template to develop a business plan in conjunction with a business plan detailed table of contents.

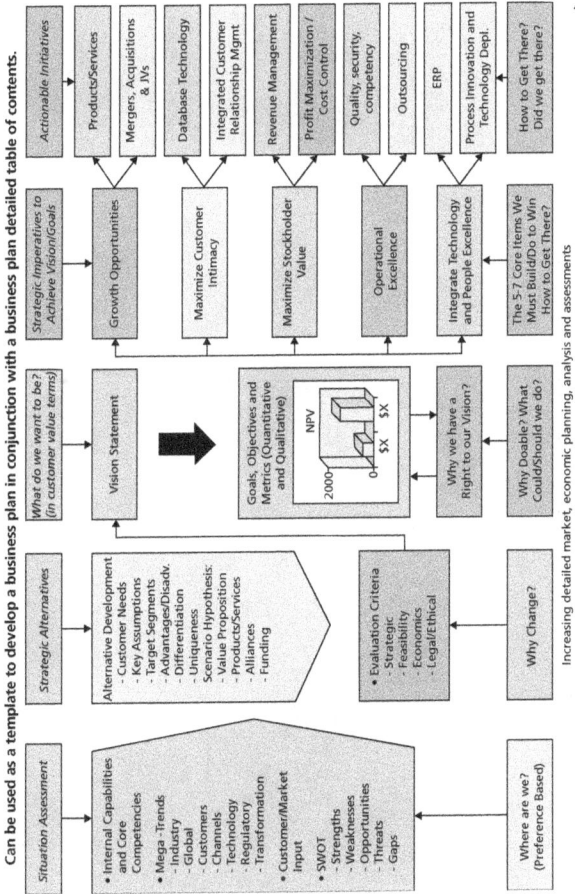

Figure 3.4 Business strategy and plan development framework

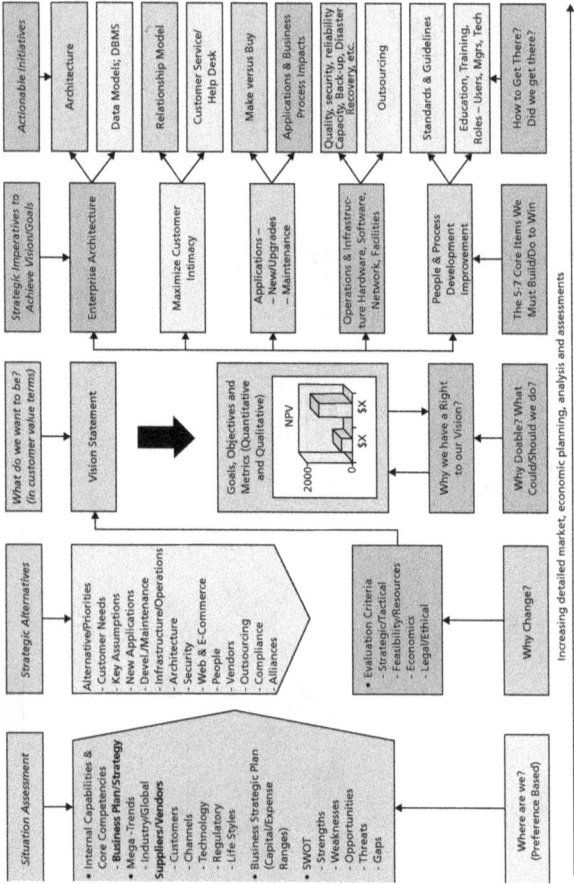

Figure 3-5 IT strategy and plan development framework

3.4 IT engagement and relationship model and roles

IT must become more customer-centric and marketing-oriented in order to develop closer and more collaborative relationships with the business. A growing number of enterprises have instituted a business and IT engagement and relationship model.

The goals of the model are to develop a strong and sustainable partnership between the business and IT. Key elements of the model include:

- **Single point or limited points of contact** – establish a single point, or limited points of contact between IT and the business, to build a better partnership, collaboration and trust between IT and the business
- **Rules of engagement** – define standard, enterprise-wide rules of engagement for acquiring IT services
- **Accountability** – clarify roles, responsibilities and accountabilities for plans, budgets, work requests and issues resolution, escalation and performance reviews within IT, and between IT and business
- **Consistent process** – improve service delivery through a consistent process for engaging the right people at the right time using a consistent set of people, process and technology

Figure 3.7 illustrates a business and IT engagement and relationship model, which can be tailored for an organization and identifies the roles of the key constituents that should be involved.

Illustrates the roles and responsibilities of the business and IT to develop a more collaborative
environment at multiple levels. This is customizable for any organization

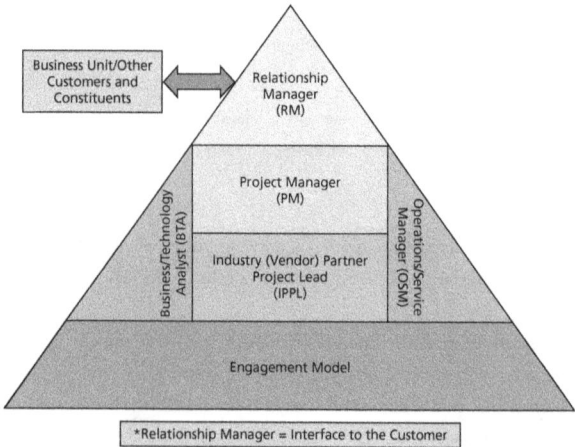

Figure 3.7 Business/IT engagement and relationship model

3.5 Summary and key take aways

Summary

IT/business alignment is complex, multi-dimensional and never complete.
However, there are IT/business alignment principles (eg planning,
investment portfolio management, relationship model, steering and
governance boards, etc.) that, if implemented, will help to achieve a more
effective and collaborative alignment.

Therefore, it is important not only to focus on measurements based
on value realization (eg quantitative), but also to take into account the
enterprise's performance and process improvements in creating the value.

Improving IT and business alignment can be achieved by implementing formal IT governance processes and mechanisms. Improving alignment maturity, like governance, is a journey based on a dynamic process that should be continuously improved. For organizations that are at the high end of the maturity model (level 4 or 5), IT and business strategy and operational alignment is an integral part of their culture. They constantly monitor alignment through key performance metrics and other techniques on a continuous basis. Business and IT alignment will remain a major issue in some organizations, until they realize that they both need each other in order to sustain the growth and prosperity of the enterprise.

Key take aways

- Ensure that IT supports the strategies of the business by developing a strategic and operating IT plan as a full partner with the business, based on similar processes.
- Establish a practical and realistic framework for measurement and reporting the results.
- Identify value adding business activities (eg value chain and other models/attributes) and strategies that would enhance them through IT; deploy incremental deliverable and communicate the benefits achieved.
- Ensure appropriate commitment and participation of executive management and the senior management team, through steering boards and formal reviews, and link alignment objectives to performance objectives, performance evaluations and rewards.
- Establish a public relations/marketing function in IT to create awareness of the value and benefits created by IT for the organization, and to improve communications.
- A successful allocation of IT resources occurs only if multiple perspectives are evaluated and the decision is not based solely on the

passion of the advocate. Enterprises need to evaluate the financial perspective, the risk level and – most importantly – whether the project contributes to the achievement of the business objectives and adds value.

Chapter 4
Principles for managing successful organizational change, prerequisites for world class leadership and developing high performance teams

4.1 Overview

As previously discussed, effective IT governance is built on three critical pillars. One of these pillars focuses on effective and motivated leadership and change agents, building high performance teams and managing organizational change successfully.

Based on the large amount of research completed in these areas, the author has adopted and modified several principles and practices in each of the areas covered in this chapter, to make them pragmatic and actionable in helping organizations transform themselves to higher levels of IT governance maturity.

Coping with the realities of change

Formalizing and institutionalizing IT governance may require significant change in an organization, depending on its current level of maturity, culture, management philosophy, available funding and resources, time constraints, business strategy, priorities and other factors. There are a number of realities of change that organizations must take into consideration when embarking on new or major change initiatives, such as IT governance. They include:

- Change has no conscience, plays no favorites, takes no prisoners and ruthlessly destroys organizations with non-adaptive or non-innovative cultures.
- A common response to change is caution. This is wrong today. Picking up speed protects you better in today's world, to cope with constant and accelerating change. One major global organization, which uses 'lean' processes, focuses its change efforts on 'cycle time reduction'.
- Success comes from cool-headed thinking, clear focus and well aimed action. So create a culture that is steady under fire.
- Initiative must always come from individuals and not just from the company, so create a shared vision and mobilize commitment.
- Inertia is more crippling than mistakes (you should learn from mistakes). Inaction is the most costly error.
- Innovate, break out of old routines and be willing to make radical changes to improve.
- Be willing to bend and learn because in a rapidly changing world, new competencies are required.

4.2　Framework for managing accelerating change

A framework for change should be a practical and useable roadmap for managing the change that assures the conditions of the change are met well, accepted by the organization in general, and integrated into the operations and culture of the organization.

According to John Kotter, there are two necessary conditions for accelerating change successfully:

- leadership for change and changing systems, processes, structures, technologies
- capabilities that are weaved into the fabric of the organization

Kotter goes on to suggest that there are five essential elements of change:

- creating a shared need
- shaping a vision
- mobilizing commitment
- making change last
- monitor progress and continuous learning

Successful change requires strong committed leadership and a respected champion throughout the entire initiative, and also to sustain a continuous improvement effort that should be reinforced by specific actions such as:

- Let people know that the change is not an option.
- Communicate clearly that performance measures and rewards are linked to measurable improvements as a result of the change initiative.
- Make space for 'grieving' based on the old environment, but encourage 'moving on' to the new environment.
- Ensure that the change process 'conditions' and 'elements' are fulfilled.
- Lead by example, with passion, energy and the right attitude.
- Leadership cannot do it alone and in isolation - other motivated change agents must be enlisted at all levels of the organization.
- Change requires work and attention – planning, management and governance.
- Change requires supporting systems, structures, tools and training.

Figure 4.1 illustrates a framework for managing major change, used by a large financial service and insurance organization. It can be adopted and tailored for IT governance and its components, either individually or as a whole. Furthermore, Figure 4.1 also identified specific questions that should be addressed for key change elements.

Used to Help Organization Transition from the Current Environment to a Future Environment

Leading Change:
– Is there a strong change leadership team (CLT) and champion? Knowledgeable in the model and tools?
– Is the CLT actively involved in leading and driving the change process and initiatives?
– Are CLT members monitoring all 'essential elements' and 'necessary conditions'?

A Framework for Managing Change				
Creating Shared Need:	**Shaping Vision:**	**Making Commitment:**	**Making Change Endure:**	**Monitoring Progress & Learning:**
– Is the reason to change, whether driven by threat or opportunity, instilled within organization? – Is it widely shared through data, demonstration, demand or diagnosis? – Does the need for change exceed its resistance?	– Is the desired outcome of change clear, and legitimate? – Is the outcome expressed in simple terms? – Is it widely understood and shared?	– Is there a strong commitment from all key constituents to invest in the change, make it work, and demand and receive management attention?	– Once the change is started, can we implement it on a sustained basis? – Are the results transferred throughout the organization?	– Do we know our real progress? – Have benchmarks and metrics been set to guarantee accountability? – Has organization feedback and learning been captured?

Changing Systems, Structures & Capabilities:
– Is change woven into the very fabric of the organization?
– Are management practices used to complement and reinforce change?
– How have we addressed issues of: staffing & development, measurements & rewards?
– Is there a communication strategy?
– Do we know how the organizational structure must be changed?

Figure 4.1 Framework for managing change and related questions

4.3 Organizing for the IT governance initiative

An effective IT governance environment represented by level 3 or higher on the CMMI maturity model is difficult to achieve. It takes time, resources and the right skills and attitudes. The journey can be made easier by following a modified version of Kotter's eight stage process for leading change:

- **Establish a sense of urgency** – motivated by a threat or an opportunity
- **Create the guiding coalition** – identify the group and individuals that lead the change, encourage change agents to solicit broad based support, and facilitate the execution through empowerment
- **Develop a vision and strategy** – ensuring a realistic vision and supporting strategies

- **Communicate the vision and strategy** – over-communicating is good
- **Empower a broad based action** – encouraging risk-taking and overcome and/or neutralize obstacles
- **Generate short-term wins** – completing wins that are communicated to the constituents and are very effective for gaining support and sustaining the change direction
- **Consolidate gains and produce more change** – leverage increased credibility from successes, which facilitates and stimulates the introduction of more change
- **Anchor new approaches in the culture** – institutionalize the process, adapt enabling technology and tools, and link progress to performance

The following activities will further help to organize a successful IT governance initiative:

- identify executive champion and multi-disciplinary team (to focus on each major IT governance component)
- do your homework – get up-to-date on current and emerging best practices
- market and communicate the IT governance value proposition
- develop a tailored IT governance framework and roadmap for your organization based on current and emerging industry best practices
- decompose the IT governance components into well defined work packages (assign an owner and champion to each process component)
- assess the 'current state' of the level of IT governance maturity
- develop a 'future state' IT governance blueprint (where you want to be) and keep it in focus
- develop an IT governance action plan, identify deliverables, establish priorities, milestones and allocate resources
- identify enabling technologies to support the IT governance initiative

4.4 World class leadership principles and practices

The success of major enterprise initiatives like IT governance is more often determined by people or 'soft' skills, such as leadership communications, integrity, persistence, judgment, managing expectations, inter-personal, team building and managing change and innovation skills, performed well, rather than by 'hard' skills, such as plans, procedures, processes and technologies.

Most world class organizations develop leadership and management succession plans that are based on a specific set of skills and competencies. Figure 4.2 represents a blend of the major skills and competencies required for leadership positions in these companies. They are broken into five areas:

- leadership
- marketing and customer focus
- critical thinking
- achieving results and effective execution
- functional expertise

These can apply to IT governance as well as to many other enterprise initiatives.

One CIO's rules for IT service and governance

Many CIOs today have created their own set of leadership and management rules, written them down, distributed them to their organization and integrated them into the daily life of the organization. Some lists are very specific, covering such areas as governance, alignment, compliance and capital expenditures, while others relate to actionable principles.

The Leadership Competency Model represents a blend of models developed by select leading edge organizations such as Verizon, Motorola, Proctor and Gamble, GE and Others

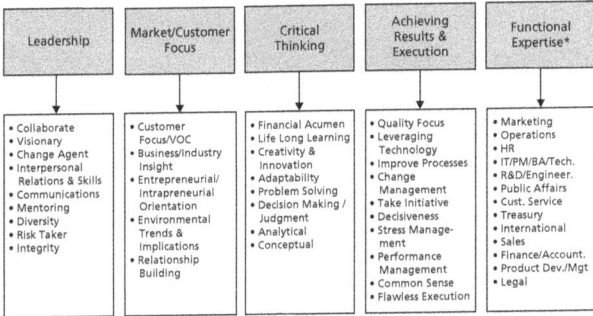

Leadership	Market/Customer Focus	Critical Thinking	Achieving Results & Execution	Functional Expertise*
• Collaborate • Visionary • Change Agent • Interpersonal Relations & Skills • Communications • Mentoring • Diversity • Risk Taker • Integrity	• Customer Focus/VOC • Business/Industry Insight • Entrepreneurial/ Intrapreneurial Orientation • Environmental Trends & Implications • Relationship Building	• Financial Acumen • Life Long Learning • Creativity & Innovation • Adaptability • Problem Solving • Decision Making / Judgment • Analytical • Conceptual	• Quality Focus • Leveraging Technology • Improve Processes • Change Management • Take Initiative • Decisiveness • Stress Management • Performance Management • Common Sense • Flawless Execution	• Marketing • Operations • HR • IT/PM/BA/Tech. • R&D/Engineer. • Public Affairs • Cust. Service • Treasury • International • Sales • Finance/Account. • Product Dev./Mgt • Legal

Figure 4.2 The leadership competency model

Bill Godfrey, CIO of Dow Jones, developed a set of rules that, '... *in one form or another are there to sustain, protect and foster alignment ...*' (Wailgum, 2005).

Godfrey's fourteen 'big rules' for IT service and governance are:

Rule 1 – Strategic planning
- All technology divisions will have a documented technology plan.
- All technology divisions will have published goals and objectives.

Rule 2 – Production prioritization
- Production problems classified as 'severity one' production problems take resource precedent over all else. Management and staff will work on 'severity one' problems immediately and continually until resolved.

Rule 3 – Enterprise architecture
- All technology divisions will have a documented high level architecture.
- All technology divisions will adhere to infrastructure standards or seek exception approval.

- All technology projects costing more than $250,000 in total must be approved through an 'early look' screening process prior to capital approval submission.

Rule 4 – Project management

- There will be 100% adherence to the project management process for all non-trivial development projects (projects estimated to take more than two weeks of staff time).
- All development projects will have a specifically identified business sponsor and a specifically identified IT project leader prior to initiation.
- All development projects requiring infrastructure support will directly involve infrastructure support staff during project initiation, giving the infrastructure staff an opportunity to directly participate in the design of systems solutions.

Rule 5 – Time management

- All staff time will be appropriately entered into the IT time reporting system on a weekly basis.

Rule 6 – Technology business management

- As represented in approved budgets, technology costs will not exceed plan unless explicit approval is granted by the CIO.
- Technology contracts will be managed and approved through business management services or purchasing.
- All third-party contractors and consultants will sign non-disclosure agreements, managed under the non-employee security policy, and managed through the company's preferred vendor program.

Rule 7 – Capital approval management

- All projects will adhere to corporate expenditure authorization processes.
- All projects are required to have appropriate IT senior leadership team sign-offs prior to business line submission.

- For all projects requiring CIO approval, all staff work and IT senior leadership team approvals will be complete prior to seeking CIO approval.
- Any project with a total cost of more than $250,000 will be submitted to finance for formal business case review.

Rule 8 – Requesting proposals from third parties

- All requests for proposals from third parties will be reviewed and approved by the CIO prior to execution.
- All requests for proposals from third parties which could have infrastructure implications will be reviewed and approved by IT infrastructure services prior to execution.

Rule 9 – Relationship management

- Business technology directors are 100% accountable for all technology, direct and indirect, in support of their assigned business lines.
- Business technology directors 'own' all business application vendor relationships.
- Enterprises technology directors 'own' all infrastructure vendor relationships.

Rule 10 – Infrastructure management

- Enterprise infrastructure services are 100% accountable for the global infrastructure.
- Enterprise infrastructure services are the only organization that makes infrastructure decisions.
- Enterprise infrastructure services own and manage all infrastructure capital.

Rule 11 – Compliance with audit, regulatory and legal requirements

- Information technology services will comply will all audit, regulatory and legal requirements.
- The IT senior leadership team is accountable for compliance.

Rule 12 – Operations procedural compliance

- There will be 100% compliance with [the] enterprise change control policy and procedure.
- All production applications will be supported by a service level agreement between IT and the business.

Rule 13 – Information security

- All technology staff will comply with the company's information security policy.
- Information security approval must be secured prior to implementing new technology or making major enhancements to existing technology. This review and approval is to take place before any informal or formal obligations are made between the company and a supplier.
- All access to a financially significant application will be managed and controlled through information security.

Rule 14 – Sarbanes-Oxley compliance

- There will be 100% compliance to all Sarbanes-Oxley controls.
- All IT leaders will be thoroughly familiar with the IT general control policies regarding governance, project management, operations, access control and data management.
- All IT leaders, supervisor and above, are responsible and accountable for Sarbanes-Oxley compliance across their respective areas of control.

4.5 Principles for creating and sustaining high performance teams

Many companies, such as Haliburton, Quaker Oats, TRW and General Mills, who have established effective team environments and culture, reported a 20-40% gain in productivity after 12–18 months (Johnson, 2002).

Organizations are developing increasingly complex team-based organizational structures to (Snyder, 2003; Katzenback and Smith, 2001; Lohr, 2007):

- address constantly changing business needs, that compel organizational structures to be fluid and where team members can be moved to where their expertise is required
- build a successful organization of the future (which is now); a few guiding principles should guide that effort:

  - organize for continuous change; stability is out and 'organizational whitewater' is in
  - develop and support knowledge workers; the person(s) whose intellectual capital will fuel future innovation
  - harvest global brains; national boundaries are no longer barriers to innovation; global 'centers of excellence', focusing on different IT competencies, have and are being set up by companies such as IBM, Toyota, Cisco, Tata and others
  - enable networks of cross-specialization experts; silos and smokestacks are dying; future success will depend on how efficiently a company links its 'centers of excellence' to create value and share learning, independent of location

According to Snyder, the characteristics of world class team members include (Snyder, 2003):

- represent inter-disciplinary and cross-functional business units
- either serve in a full-time assignment reporting directly to a team leader, or report part-time to team leaders and part-time to their functional bosses, as in a matrix organization
- can be co-located or work at different locations, virtually
- are knowledge workers

For enterprise governance to improve the bottom line, well-lead multi-disciplinary and cross-functional teams must be established with wide representation from the business and IT. A team represents a collection of people who rely on group collaboration, such that each of the team members experiences an optimum level of success, achieving both personal and team-based goals and objectives.

A team chartered to develop an IT governance initiative and plan should include the CIO (as the champion), his or her direct reports, and have representation from both key business units and corporate staff functions (such as finance, audit, operations, legal and the executive office). The various working committee(s), responsible for developing and deploying the key IT governance components, should be composed of staff from areas such as alignment, planning, program and project management, IT Service Management, strategic sourcing, performance management and controls and audit.

Building blocks for team development and effectiveness

Teams represent a form of organization. Most organizations function with some form of structure, rules and processes. Effective world class teams also require building blocks and guidelines to work smartly. These include some of the following:

- **Goals** – are clear to all, challenging, yet realistic; each individual's work relates to overall team goals and objectives.
- **Roles** – are mutually understood; everyone knows why they are on the team; authority and responsibilities are consistent.
- **Boundaries** – describe the scope and parameters of what the team is empowered to do, and what is off-limits.
- **Processes** exist - with key processes in place to support the work of the team:

- problem-solving and issue identification
- planning, decision-making and authority
- handling conflict, resolution or escalation
- managing expectations of constituents
- contents, format and frequent of communications
- meeting management – agendas, minutes, follow-up actions
- resource management and allocation
- team training and new team member absorption
- evaluation of team effectiveness and performance
- team dissolution and reassignment of team members
- interactions with other teams and organizations

- **Relationships** - team members communicate openly and demonstrate trust for one another; the team establishes relationships beyond itself (external touch points), as needed in the organization.

The first critical step in developing high performance teams is to 'set them up for success'. Senior management and other key stakeholders (or the team itself, if it a self-directed team) should hold planning discussions to reach consensus on such issues as:

- the team's purpose, charter, boundaries, scope and expected outcomes
- the team's structure, team leader (individual or shared or self directed) and team members
- strategies for management commitment, support, resource allocation and issues escalation
- the team's measures of success, key performance indicators and their links to MBO (management by objectives), compensation and incentives
- the team's rules and processes for communications, progress reporting, meetings, conflict-resolution, problem and issues workouts, self-assessment, managing expectations of stakeholders, etc.

Figure 4.3 summarizes a list of operating characteristics generally present in effective high performance teams.

Clear Purpose	The vision, mission, goal or task of the team has been defined and is now accepted by everyone. There is an action plan.
Informality	The climate tends to be informal, comfortable, and relaxed. There are no obvious tensions or signs of boredom.
Participation	There is much discussion and everyone is encouraged to participate.
Listening	The members use effective listening techniques such as questioning, paraphrasing and summarizing to get ideas out.
Civilized Disagreement	There is disagreement, but the team is comfortable with this and shows no signs of avoiding, smoothing over, or suppressing conflict.
Consensus and Fast Decisions	For important decisions, the goal is substantial but not necessarily unanimous agreement through open discussion of everyone's ideas, avoidance of formal voting, or easy compromises. It is also important to avoid or minimize 'groupthink' which often limits individual creativity and may sub-optimize the team's actions.
Open communication	Team members feel free to express their feelings on the tasks as well as on the group's operation. There are few hidden agendas. Communication takes place outside of meetings.
Clear Roles and Work Assignments	There are clear expectations about roles played by each team member. When action is taken, clear assignments are made, accepted and carried out. Work is fairly distributed among members.
Shared Leadership	While the team has a formal leader, leadership functions shift from time to time depending upon the circumstances, the needs of the group, and the skills of the members. The former leader models the appropriate behavior and helps establish positive norms.
External Relations	The team spends time developing key outside relationships, mobilizing resources, and building credibility with important players in other parts of the organization.
Style and Cultural Diversity	The team has a broad spectrum of team-player types representing different cultures including members who emphasize attention to task, goal setting, focus on process and questions about how the team is functioning.
Self-Assessment	Periodically, the team steps back to examine how well it is functioning, examines what may be interfering with its effectiveness and takes corrective actions.
Use of Technology	Organizations are creating 'global centers of excellence' to take advantage of global brains. This has accelerated the use of technology to save time, costs and facilitate collaboration amongst multi-location team members.

Figure 4.3 Summary of operating characteristics present in world class teams

Select technologies for teams

As organizations become more global, they are establishing 'centers of excellence' in many parts of the world, to take advantage of global brains, reduced labor rates, unique and specialized skills, rare resources and, perhaps, more lax regulatory environments than exist in their home base.

Technologies used by teams generally improve communications and collaboration, increase decision-making speed and time to market, reduce costs and take advantage of a twenty-four hour work day. In addition, as organizations increase their outsourcing expenditures, technology is playing a growing and increasing important role in connecting the customers with their service providers and suppliers. Figure 4.4 provides examples of select technologies used by traditional and virtual teams, based in the same or different geographic locations and/or time zones.

Technologies used by teams generally improve communications and collaboration, increase decision-making speed and reduce costs.

Technologies for Teams:

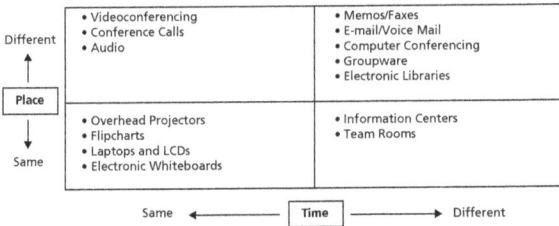

Place	Same Time	Different Time
Different	• Videoconferencing • Conference Calls • Audio	• Memos/Faxes • E-mail/Voice Mail • Computer Conferencing • Groupware • Electronic Libraries
Same	• Overhead Projectors • Flipcharts • Laptops and LCDs • Electronic Whiteboards	• Information Centers • Team Rooms

Same ←——— **Time** ———→ Different

Figure 4.4 Select technologies for teams

4.6 Summary and key take aways

Summary – checklist for managing accelerating change

- define the change – create a common understanding of the change
- build company capacity – change management skills, resources and roles (champion, sponsors, agents, targets)
- assess the climate – implementation history and stress levels

- generate sponsorship – construct , cascade and sponsor role
- get the right talent - with the right skills and attitudes
- determine change approach - commitment or compliance
- develop target readiness – identify and manage resistance to change at all levels and determine how to overcome it
- develop communications plan – communicate in terms of frame of reference
- develop reinforcement strategy – align rewards and efforts required to achieve IT governance objectives, and measure results
- create cultural fit – identify conflicts and unwritten rules
- prioritize action – a project plan
- evaluate the change process
- reward significant progress – link incentive pay and other rewards to quantifiable objectives

Summary – checklist for leadership and effective teams

- clear purpose, common vision and accountability
- obsession with external customer
- participation and well defined roles
- civilized disagreement and style diversity – allow for workout meetings and discussions
- encourage open communications – silence is consent – voice your ideas
- encourage flexible discipline and even expulsion of non-productive team members
- blend of informality and formality
- focus on both process and end results; however, remember that results are more important than process
- acknowledgement of the need for change
- strong respect and trust between members and leaders
- single point of contact for official team progress and communications (do not feed rumour-mill)

- self-assessment of team members and adjustment
- no ideas are bad ideas; encourage 'no blame game'
- use automated tools to increase speed and communications

Key take aways

Steven Covey identified the **seven habits of highly effective people**. These not only impact on how well individuals perform, but also on how well organizations and teams perform.

These habits represent 'superior take aways' from this chapter (Covey, 1989):

- **be proactive** – take the initiative; act or be acted upon
- **begin with the end in mind** – vision, mission, scope, deliverables and boundaries
- **put first things first** – time bounds; time management (A,B,C); prioritize
- **think and act 'win-win'** – everyone wins if the team wins – individuals, team members, leaders and organization
- **seek first to understand, then to be understood** – active listening; diagnose before you prescribe
- **synergize** – creative collaboration and innovation; value differences
- **'sharpen the saw'** – continuous learning and renewal; adopt best practices; create a knowledge management database of lessons learned (good and bad) – enable easy access to them

Chapter 5
Program and project management excellence (execution management)

5.1 Overview

Program and project management is a major component of effective IT governance that focuses on execution management.

The focus of this chapter is to provide a blend of frameworks, checklists, tools, templates, techniques and metrics to help deliver programs and projects on time, within scope, within budget, with high quality and to the customer's satisfaction or, get them back on track. It suggests a scalable and flexible PM life cycle framework, based on a blend of best practices that can be tailored to handle different project types (eg simple, moderate and complex).

Why is program/project management important?

The objective of project management is to make the most effective use of multiple resources by delivering projects on time, on budget, within scope, with high quality, to the customer's satisfaction, with a minimum of or no rework, and the mitigation of the major risks. The resources include personnel, equipment, facilities, materials, capital, technology, external resources (eg suppliers and service providers), intellectual property and other assets.

As all kinds of programs and projects become more pervasive in organizations, to manage a wide range of initiatives (such as new product development, mergers and acquisitions, new or updates to enterprise-wide information systems, new building and facilities construction and others), both private and public sector leaders have recognized that project management is a strategic imperative. Project management provides organizations and people with a powerful set of processes, tools and technologies that improve their ability to plan, implement, integrate and manage activities to meet business objectives. Project management is a results-oriented management discipline that places a high value on building collaborative relationships among a diverse set of people located anywhere to complete specific deliverables.

Project management skills and competencies

As the complexity of projects increase, the project manager and team must have a broad range of skills and competencies to be effective. Figure 5.1 identifies the skills and competencies required in the complex and fast paced project environments of the future.

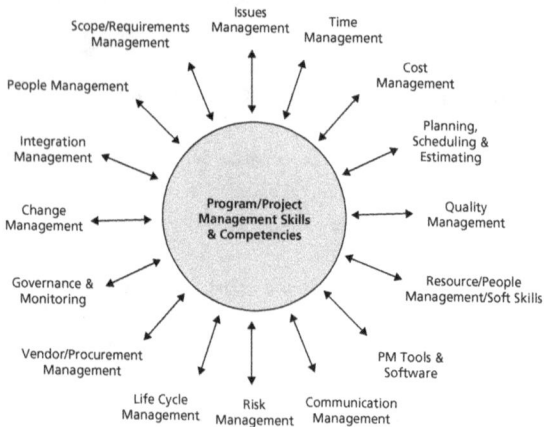

Figure 5.1 Project management is complex and requires multiple skills and competencies

The five 'W's and 2 'H's of project management

Early on, it is important to establish the basic questions that will help to define the parameters of a program or project. The fundamental questions that help to scope a project include:

- **Why** ... are we doing this? Are we solving a newly discovered problem, fixing an existing problem, pursuing an opportunity, cutting costs, increasing revenues, or increasing productivity? Everyone, from top to bottom, must know the answer, and the answer must be on this list.

- **Who** ... wants this done? Is it an executive sponsor, project task force/project manager and team, owner(s) of deliverables, customers or outside stakeholders? Has that person/team sold the 'why' and assumed responsibility and commitment from key people?

- **What** ... are the details? Is the project feasible? Is it linked to the organization's vision and plan? Are all the resources (human, financial, material, facilities, etc.) available and committed? Have the project's scope and objectives been approved and sold to all? Have risks been evaluated and contingencies planned for? Have interface and integration concerns been addressed?

- **How** ... will we do this? How much will be built? How much bought? How much will be outsourced? How will we audit outsourced progress/quality? How will problems be addressed and escalated?

- **When** ... are deliverables required? Are deadlines, schedules, milestones and critical path tasks identified, and are all involved aware of them?

- **Where** ... will this be done and where are the affected stakeholders? Where are the departments, functions, locations, countries and people?

- **How much** … is the budget? How much has been budgeted, committed, allocated and spent? How will we measure the performance and key metrics? How will any variances between budgets, actuals and baselines be addressed?

5.2 Project management is complex, but has significant value

Major causes of program/project failures and challenges

There are many reasons for program and project failures and challenges. Major reasons include:

- lack of, or poor, business case
- lack of executive commitment, visibility and accountability
- poorly defined requirements, scope, objectives and deliverables
- poor communications
- failure to treat projects as a start-up initiative
- unrealistic expectations
- limited constituent involvement and ownership
- lack of, or insufficient, and the right kind of, resources
- lack of, or poor integration within the, organization (and to other systems)
- no plan, no risk assessment and mitigation, no contingency plan alternatives
- lack of measurable controls and metrics
- ineffective implementation strategy
- underestimation of project complexity, costs and time
- poor or unreliable vendor deliverables
- lack of training for either the project team, or those constituents who are impacted by the project

- inflexible, limited or no project management process
- poor use or over-reliance on the use of project management tools and software

The cost of program and project management failure

Both the Standish Group and Gartner have conducted periodic annual surveys on the state of project management in the USA. These surveys divide programs and projects into three classifications – failed, challenged and successful.

- **Failed:** The first class represents failed projects that have been started, but never finished for a variety of reasons – the sponsor resigned, the need went away, poor requirements definition, avoiding a disaster about to happen and scope creep.
- **Challenged:** The second class represents challenged projects, which have been implemented, but with one or more significant challenges, such as over budget, over schedule, under scoped and rework due to changing requirements.
- **Successful:** The third class represents successful projects that have been implemented, generally on time, within budget, within scope, with reasonable quality and to the customer's satisfaction.

According to a blend of Standish and Gartner surveys, the estimated annual cost range of failed and challenged projects in the USA is $100 to 150 billion. Figure 5.2 illustrates these numbers for small, medium and large organizations.

Questions that the author asks senior executives of companies regarding their project environments include:

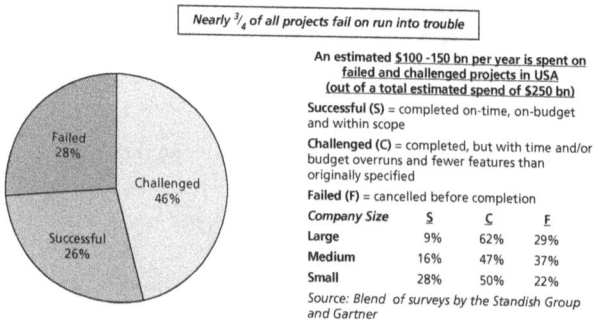

Nearly ³/₄ of all projects fail on run into trouble

An estimated $100 -150 bn per year is spent on failed and challenged projects in USA (out of a total estimated spend of $250 bn)

Successful (S) = completed on-time, on-budget and within scope

Challenged (C) = completed, but with time and/or budget overruns and fewer features than originally specified

Failed (F) = cancelled before completion

Company Size	S	C	F
Large	9%	62%	29%
Medium	16%	47%	37%
Small	28%	50%	22%

Source: Blend of surveys by the Standish Group and Gartner

Figure 5.2 The cost of project management failure

- How much of these costs are contributed by your organization?
- Do you really have a good grasp of this kind of information?
- How effective are your organization's project management governance policies, frameworks, standards, processes, tools, disciplines and training programs?

More often than not, senior executives do not have readily available answers to these questions. That is part of the problem, and can also become part of the solution. This information, or lack thereof, can be used to ignite specific actions in organizations, by creating greater awareness of the impact on lower profitability due to poor project management practices, and rallying the troops to a call-to-action, to improve the effectiveness of the project and organization environment and adding value.

5.3 Principles for achieving excellence in program/project management

Key attributes of successful program- and project-based organizational cultures and environments

Based on many of the case studies analyzed, a review of the literature and numerous consulting assignments, it is clear that organizations continue to struggle with establishing and enforcing a formal program/project management policy and process that is sustainable. In addition, a number of key project management principles and practices were identified and consistently applied, for the most part, by leading-edge, successful organizations (Selig, September 2004).

These principles and practices can represent a checklist for helping companies achieve improvements, and higher levels of project management maturity and effectiveness, in their environments. They have been organized into logical categories to facilitate their use.

Program/project management excellence and visibility:

- Top management must prioritize projects based on consistent and repeatable evaluation and selection processes.
- Customers must approve and set priorities among projects.
- Implement projects successfully (eg on-time, on-budget, within scope, with high quality and to the customers satisfaction).
- The CEO (eg CIO; CFO; CMO; COO; etc.) is committed to implementing project management as a core competency to manage all types of projects.
- Conduct formal periodic project management assessments and reviews with senior management.

- Projects must be limited to a size that can be fully understood by the project manager.
- Successful project management must be a joint effort between customers and the project teams. But the final responsibility for success or failure lies with the customer.
- Market and communicate the benefits and positive results of good fundamental project management disciplines through newsletters, websites, word of mouth, customer testimonials and other promotion vehicles.
- Develop a business case for major complex and moderate projects (defined later in this chapter).
- An essential element of every project is a complete project plan based on a work break down structure, with assignable work packages, task identification, estimating, budgeting and scheduling.
- Planning is everything and ongoing – detailed, systematic and team-involved.
- What is not documented has not been said or does not exist.
- The more ridiculous the deadline, the more it costs to try to meet it.
- Project sponsors and constituents must be active participants – this builds relationships, communications and commitment.
- Use industry standards and guidelines to guide your project management direction - CMMI, PMMM, ISO 9000, PRINCE2, Six Sigma, Baldrige and others.

Sponsorship, accountability and leadership:

- All programs/projects must have a sponsor and/or owner and an overall program/project manager.
- Key roles and responsibilities must be formally agreed to upfront, and communicated to all of the constituencies where individuals are assigned specific actions in the form of a **RACI** matrix (**R**esponsible, **A**pprove, **C**onsult, **I**nform) which becomes part of the project documentation.

- Program/project scope, requirements and deliverables should be approved upfront by the sponsor.
- Program/project costs and benefits (including non-financial benefits) should be quantified and approved by the sponsor and charged back to the sponsor or owner.
- Fast projects have strong leaders who create a sense of urgency and speed.
- Professionalize project management, reward certification and celebrate successes.
- Program/project scope, requirements and deliverables (as in a charter) should be approved upfront by the sponsor and monitored throughout the life cycle phases.
- The creation of a program management office (PMO) is important, to act as a 'center of excellence' to develop and maintain project management processes, co-ordinate training and certification, manage or consult on select large projects or those projects in trouble and facilitate project planning, status reporting and periodic formal reviews.
- Project Managers must focus on five dimensions of project success – on time, within budget, within scope, with acceptable quality and to the customer's satisfaction.
- Project life cycle with 'go/no go' gates allows for mid-course project reviews and adjustments and/or cancellations.
- A project manager's most valuable and least used word is 'no'.
- The same work under the same conditions will be estimated differently by five different estimators or by one estimator five different times.
- Project manager responsibility must be matched by equivalent authority.
- Projects management must be sold and resold via the value propositions.
- Project team members deserve a clear, written charter and guidelines as to the tasks they must perform and the time available to perform them.
- Questions generated by the project team deserve direct answers from the customer.
- Great project managers do not encourage burnout.

- Establish project review panels, consisting of key constituents, and conduct formal reviews with follow-up actions, dates and assigned responsibility.
- Use outside subject matter project management experts as needed.

Program/project management (PM) governance policy, change control and escalation

Key practices for successful and sustainable superior project management best practices include the following:

- A formal project management governance policy should be established, defining the components of the policy, and identify what is mandatory and discretionary, and who has decision authority for approval, resource allocation, escalation and change authorization.
- A formal governance calendar should be published, which identifies formal project reviews, status reports (eg weekly, bi-weekly, monthly, quarterly), funding reviews, etc.
- A flexible and scalable project management process should be established and continuously improved to accommodate different project types.
- A project management 'center of excellence' (PMO) should be established to develop criteria for project management competencies, encourage project management training and certification, provide expert project management help, act as project management advocates and conduct periodic health checks on select programs/projects.
- Establish a reward and recognition system to recognize project management excellence and encourage certification.
- Supply short-term incremental project deliverables that work to establish credibility and visibility (decompose complex programs and projects into no more than 80 hour work packages with targeted deliverables, formal project reviews, etc.). Shorter work packages based on 40 hours or less are also acceptable for priority projects.

- Incorporate project management objectives into annual performance reviews.
- Consistent program and project metrics should be instituted, based on time, cost, resources, quality and customer satisfaction (including earned value, where applicable). There are a number of tools that can help with estimating, resource allocation, level loading and resource utilization.
- The ability to compare planned to actual results or base lines is essential for effective project management.
- Management must be provided meaningful visibility into projects if suspicion and distrust are to be minimized.
- The key to good project management is effective and honest communications.
- A formal escalation process, with clear accountability and roles should be established to resolve key program/project issues, risks and approve changes.
- A consistent methodology must be developed and applied to report the **RAG** (eg **R**ed, **A**mber or **G**reen status of programs, projects or other major tasks: Red = significant trouble; Amber = emerging trouble; Green = everything is on target).
- Reporting must be produced on a consistent basis (eg weekly, bi-weekly, monthly, other) using a consistent format (eg with allowances made for the audience of the report).
- A formal time tracking system should be in place to record how time is spent on projects.
- A formal link, including rework to the change management process, must be established to manage and monitor significant changes to budgets, schedules, versions and/or documentation.

Resource optimization, availability and commitment:
- Sponsors and program/project managers should have access to the right resources, based on the project phase, task requirements and competencies needed.

- The availability and commitment of the resources should be guaranteed by senior management once the program/project is approved and resourced.

Program/project repository and lessons learned:
- Lessons learned should be developed and made available to all constituencies who require them, with consideration given to security and access policies.
- Current and evolving best practice benchmarking should be tracked and adopted.
- Maintain a project management knowledge management system, of lessons learned and lessons to be changed.
- Desirable work must be rewarded; undesirable work must be changed.

Project management life cycle phases and key components

Programs and projects are, by definition, one time events, with a start and end date. Therefore, all projects have a life cycle. Life cycles may vary by project. For example, the life cycle of a new product development project is somewhat different to a project life cycle for an information system or merger and acquisition. In addition, PMI's PMBOK® identifies five project phases:

- initiation
- planning
- execution
- control
- termination or closure

Other project life cycles may have more or less phases. As a practical matter, the actual number of life cycle phases that a company uses is of less importance than ensuring that there is agreement that a project life cycle process, with specific phases and components, is used on a consistent, but scalable basis.

To keep things simple, Figure 5.3 represents a project management life cycle, based on four phases – initiation, planning, execution and termination. Like many other project management professionals, the author believes that 'control' is not really a separate phase in the life cycle, but rather, is an integral part of all of the life cycle phases. The actual number of phases is not as important as ensuring that a project life cycle being adopted and consistently applied, and that the value of the life cycle itself is recognized in an organization. The benefits of a project life cycle include:

- creates visibility and a roadmap through phase approvals
- establishes uniform and consistent phases
- disciplines and structures the process
- forces incremental 'go/no go' decisions at gate reviews
- forces early attention to details
- has a beginning and an end
- establishes project planning and control mechanisms
- accommodates change and risk
- creates a framework for improved communications, commitment, buy-in and visibility
- facilitates the integration of the program/project results and deliverables into the organization's core businesses, related systems, infrastructure and culture

Figure 5.3 also identifies the key components of each of the phases. Not every component must or should be used for every project, but it provides a checklist that can be applied to either light (fast track or simple), moderate or complex projects, which are discussed in more detail in Section 5.5.

INITIATING	PLANNING	EXECUTING	CLOSING & TERMINATION
• Business Need/Case • Feasibility • Authorization • Funding • Project Charter • Project Organization • Project Management Office (PMO) • Critical Success Factors • Project Metrics & Vital Signs • Go/No Go Gate	• Requirements & Scope • Objectives • Deliverables • Work Breakdown Structure • Stakeholders • Assumptions & Constraints • Estimates-Costs, Resources, Effort & Time • Sequence Tasks • Schedule • Resources • Roles, Responsibilities & Staffing Plan • Quality Management Plan • Risk/Contingency Management Plan • Disaster Recovery Plan • Change Management Plan • Communications Management Plan • Acceptance Management Plan • Integrated Project Plan (of multiple inter-related projects) • Vendor/Outsourcing Plan • Go/No Go gate	• Executing the Plan & Delivery (eg SDLC; IDLC, PMLC, Outsourcing) • Governance Structure & Escalation • Developing the Team (separate module) • Progress Reporting, Communications & Meeting Management • Comparison of Metrics & Vital Sign Baseline to Actuals • Education & Training • Vendor/Outsourcing Management • Change Control • Risk Control • Quality Control • Transition to Customer, Operations, etc.	• Project Acceptance & Approval • Complete Project Files & Documentation • Post Mortem Review & Follow-Up (1 month, 3 months, 6 months) • Lessons Learned to be Re-enforced or Changed • Finalize Project File • Administrative & Contract Closure • Reassign Project Team • Settle final accounts

> Enterprises must develop repeatable, consistent, but yet scalable & flexible PM processes to fit different types & sizes of programs and projects (eg Light versus Complex)

> Governance & Control Spans all Phases

Figure 5.3 Project management life cycle phases and key components

5.4   Making the choice – program and project management light or complex

Program/project type/scale matrix

Once a program or project is approved, a critical question asked by many is, *'how much project management process and documentation is required for this project and what project management path should be used?'*

Best practice companies, like IBM, GE, Boeing, Bechtel and others, have developed very detailed, robust and scalable project management methodologies, that are repeatable and can be consistently applied to a wide variety of projects on a global basis.

Since all programs and projects are not equal, organizations are increasingly implementing a flexible and scalable program and project management life cycle, consisting of multiple paths, such as fast track or light versus complex process, with the associated checklists and supporting tools. A growing number of organizations have developed the equivalent of a 'Chinese menu' ('choose from either column A and/or B'), to provide more choices within a broad framework of project management best practices, where the project manager and the team either get to pick the project management process, within an overall framework established by the organization, or are required to adhere to a particular path because of contractual or compliance requirements. This is how the term 'fast track or light' versus complex project management evolved, and it also helped to overcome the often-heard complaint that project management requires substantial documentation.

One method, which provides a consistent way to help select the appropriate project management process path for organizations to follow in managing their projects, is to create a project type-scale matrix. Figure 5.4 illustrates the project type-scale matrix. It provides a structured approach to determine the appropriate project management templates (and documentation) to use, to plan, manage, monitor and control a program or project throughout its life cycle phases. In essence, the project-type-scale matrix identifies the level of project management documentation required for three types of projects – simple, moderate and complex. It has been designed as a guideline to help organizations provide flexibility and choice, but within a consistent and repeatable framework.

Figure 5.4 identifies eleven complexity factors on the vertical axis and accommodates three value ratings, ranging from a low of 1 to a high of 5. Each of the eleven elements is ranked, and the total numeric value is summarized. At the bottom of the matrix, there is a point guide as to which projects are classified as simple, moderate or complex. It suggests

[Insert PROJECT # - NAME]

The Project Type/Scale Matrix provides a structured and consistent approach to determine the appropriate PM Template(s) for managing/monitoring/controlling a program/project.

PROJECT TYPE/SCALE ASSESSMENT

Directions: Calculate the matrix score by subjectively using the guidelines below to assign a number between 1 and 5 to each of the 11 factors.

	COMPLEXITY FACTOR	LOW=1	MED = 3	HIGH = 5	NOTES	ENTER SCORE (1,3 or 5)
1	Project Type	UPGRADE Involves a change in capacity of existing technology or service. Usually additional capacity or additional location	NEW ADDITION Involves the addition of a new technology or service with no replacement of existing technology or service	REPLACEMENT Involves the replacement of old technology or service with a new technology or service	*Degree of difficulty influenced by new technology and whether it replaces older technology or is simply added to the environment*	
2	Technology	Established company standard	A standard in the industry, but new to FTS	A new technology, not necessarily a standard, no internal expertise.	*Open standards should be encouraged*	
3	Scope	Involves only one location and one function	Involves only one region and up to four functions	Involves all regions (locations) and cross-functional	*The wider the geographic scope the more complex the project*	
4	End User Impact	Completely transparent to end users	Minimal amount of communication necessary to inform end users of planned changes. No training required	Changes require frequent communication and some degree of end user training		
5	Implementation technique	Can be implemented without disturbing existing service, users can migrate to new environment	New technology/service is installed in parallel and users are migrated in segments.	'Flash cut' requires new technology/service to replace old with no overlap.		
6	Capital Required (Life Cycle)	Relatively small capital (<$50k)	Medium capital required ($50k - $2.5 million)	Large capital required (>$2.5 mil)		

Figure 5.4 Program/project type-scale matrix

	Operating Costs (Annual)*	Small operating costs (< $100k/yr)	Medium operating cost ($101k-$999k/yr)	Large operating cost ($>1.0 mil/yr)	Includes depreciation, equipment lease, maintenance, etc.
7	Operating Costs (Annual)*	Small operating costs (< $100k/yr)	Medium operating cost ($101k-$999k/yr)	Large operating cost ($>1.0 mil/yr)	Includes depreciation, equipment lease, maintenance, etc.
8	Vendor relationship	No new vendors involved, upgrade using existing vendor product	No new vendor involved, using a new product from existing vendor.	New vendor with no prior business relationship	Established vendors are easier to do business with
9	Resource Requirements	Can be completed with use of only internal FTS resources (and industry partners)	Requires minimal resource dependency outside FTS (e.g. Phone Bridge)	Requires significant resource requirement from outside FTS and/or vendor (eg Enterprise Architecture, participation on project)	
10	Project Duration	<3 months	3-12 months	>12 months	
11	Other			Legal requirement and/or critical to business	
				TOTAL PROJECT Type/ Scale SCORE	0

TOTAL POINTS RANGE   11 to 55 Points

DEFINITIONS				
TYPE	Key Attributes	# of points	Recommended Template	Approvals
Simple	Low Complexity	Less than 20 Pts	Template - PR, PCR*	Director or Delegate
Moderate	Medium complexity	Between 20 and 35 Points	Template - PR, PIR, DTD, PCR (Others Optional)	CIO or Delegate
Complex	High visibility; AC directed; Multiple organizations affected	Greater than 35 Points	Template - All for tech. projects, otherwise TAD, IITQR, RFI opt.	ITRB or Delegate

*Assumes informal planning (additional templates are optional)

Figure 5.4 Program/project type-scale matrix

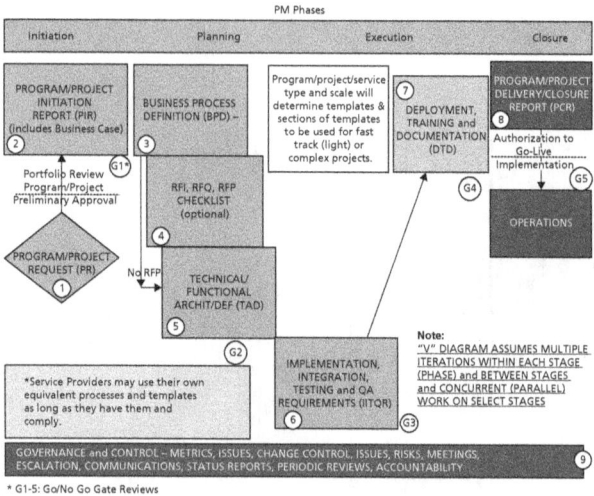

PM Phases

| Initiation | Planning | Execution | Closure |

PROGRAM/PROJECT INITIATION REPORT (PIR) (includes Business Case) (2)

BUSINESS PROCESS DEFINITION (BPD) – (3)

Program/project/service type and scale will determine templates & sections of templates to be used for fast track (light) or complex projects.

DEPLOYMENT, TRAINING and DOCUMENTATION (DTD) (7)

PROGRAM/PROJECT DELIVERY/CLOSURE REPORT (PCR) (8)

Authorization to Go-Live Implementation

Portfolio Review Program/Project Preliminary Approval   G1*

RFI, RFQ, RFP CHECKLIST (optional) (4)

(G4)

(G5)

OPERATIONS

PROGRAM/PROJECT REQUEST (PR) (1)   No RFP

TECHNICAL/ FUNCTIONAL ARCHIT/DEF (TAD) (5)

(G2)

IMPLEMENTATION, INTEGRATION, TESTING and QA REQUIREMENTS (IITQR) (6)

Note: "V" DIAGRAM ASSUMES MULTIPLE ITERATIONS WITHIN EACH STAGE (PHASE) and BETWEEN STAGES and CONCURRENT (PARALLEL) WORK ON SELECT STAGES

*Service Providers may use their own equivalent processes and templates as long as they have them and comply.

(G3)

GOVERNANCE and CONTROL – METRICS, ISSUES, CHANGE CONTROL, ISSUES, RISKS, MEETINGS, ESCALATION, COMMUNICATIONS, STATUS REPORTS, PERIODIC REVIEWS, ACCOUNTABILITY (9)

* G1-5: Go/No Go Gate Reviews

the templates that should be used for each of the project types, and the appropriate approval levels required, based on the numeric value of each project. The matrix can be tailored to different environments by changing the complexity factors, their values and respective weights.

Project management life cycle phases and related templates

The project type-scale matrix must be used in conjunction with Figure 5.5, which illustrates the project management life cycle phases, and defines the associated templates that represent the documentation required for different types of projects. The matrix identifies the recommended templates that should be used by project type. The templates are all web-based, and vary in size from one page to over ten pages. Each template also contains mandatory and discretionary information that must be completed for each project. In this way, the '*light*' (or low risk) project management

Phase(s)	Template(s)	Purpose/Description
Initiation	0. Program/Project Request (PR)	Obtains customer or other constituent authorization to request IT services
	1. Program/Project Initiation Report (PIR)	Provides sufficient high-level information on a program or project to either approve or reject the request (e.g. scope, requirements, etc.)
Planning	2. Business Project Definition (BPD)	Describes the major business objectives that the system, component or deliverable will satisfy and/or impact
	3. RFI, RFQ, RFP Checklists	Identifies the contents of a solicitation to vendors in the form of: Request for Information, Request for Quote and/or Request for Proposal
	4. Technical/Functional Architecture Definition (TAD)	Describes the complete system and/or component from a functional, technical and operational aspect
Execution**	5. Implementation, Integration, Testing and QA Requirements (IITQR)	Describes how the system and/or components is to be implemented integrated, tested and transitioned to the customer, operations and other environments
	6. Deployment, Training and Documentation (DTD)	Describes the actual installation and cutover of the system or components and identifies the training and documentation requirements
Closure	7. Program/Project Delivery/Closure Report (PCR)	Verifies and evaluates that the program/project objectives, costs, benefits and deliverables have been satisfactorily implemented and documents lessons learned

Figure 5.5 Project management life cycle phases and related templates

process can be used for *'simple'* and *'some moderate projects'* and only require the use of two templates, while *'complex'* (or high risk) projects, such as a SAP installation, would require the use of all or most of the project templates.

5.5 Program and project governance excellence

Prerequisites for effective project management execution and governance

For each project phase or major activity, the project manager should:

- review the project plan, as a reminder of the desired results of that phase or activity

- conduct a kick-off meeting, to clarify the phase deliverables, reinforce roles and responsibilities of project team members, create a shared sense of responsibility, gain commitment from the project team members, and ensure that all project team members have whatever they need to be successful in their roles
- provide authorization to project team members to start work on their activities
- conduct regular status meetings and/or provide regular status reports based on a maximum time reporting period of 80 hours (or less)
- if needed, provide training or other interventions to team members
- distribute progress reports according to a communications plan
- develop a governance and control policy, and communicate it to all project constituents

The project manager has the responsibility, during the execution phase, to compare and analyze a project's implementation progress against the baseline, and take actions to correct all significant issues and variances. This includes:

- schedule
- cost, benefits and budgets
- quality
- key deliverables
- human resources
- resource and asset allocation
- technology
- vendor deliverables

In the implementation phase, the project manager must constantly balance the monitoring, control and governance process that provides a disciplined framework to administer, monitor and control work, including:

A formal program/project review process should be established and followed with clearly defined roles and responsibilities

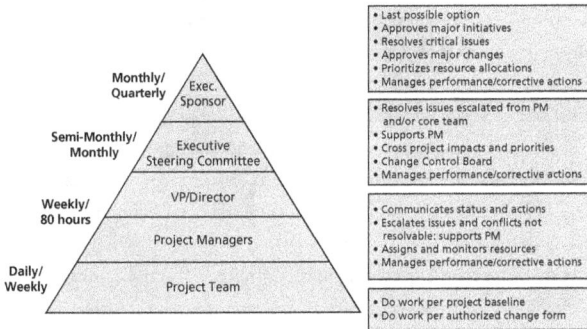

Figure 5.6 Program/project governance and escalation hierarchy

- resources (budget)
- time (start and completion dates; critical path)
- product (deliverables)
- quality
- managing expectations
- what, when and to whom to communicate

From time to time, the project manager needs help in resolving issues with difficult customers, non-supportive constituents or troublesome service providers. A formal project governance and escalation hierarchy, with clear roles and handoffs, is required. Figure 5.6 depicts such an organization.

Program management office (PMO) – roles and areas of focus

The role of the PMO is to champion project management benefit awareness, help develop project management expertise and provide administrative support (processes, tools, techniques, training, help desks) to sustain a vibrant and effective project environment in organizations. Specific PMO roles and responsibilities will vary from company to company, but can include the following:

- act as a 'center of excellence' and focal point for project management skills, competencies, methodologies, benefits and advocacy
- develop, maintain and administer all project management processes, techniques, templates and tools, to ensure effective project management implementation
- co-ordinate project management education, training and co-ordination
- establish a 'project data base repository' to enable project managers, sponsors and other constituents to plan and track the progress of all projects
- define common project management metrics and vital signs, and ensure that they are applied
- assist project managers, team members and other project constituencies to resolve project management issues, concerns and questions
- conduct select project assessment reviews
- assist with 'troubled' projects

The discipline of the 'eighty hour' rule

The '80 hour' rule facilitates project planning, scheduling, monitoring, reporting and project governance. It eliminates elastic yardsticks and subjective criteria as to monitoring project progress or lack of positive progress. There is no activity, task or event in any project which cannot be broken down into '80 hours' or less, vis-à-vis incremental deliverables, formalized project reviews and meetings, and formal status reports. There is no magic to the rule. It requires discipline, planning, thought and the ability to think in terms of decomposing projects into manageable and assignable work packages. It should be applied in the planning phase, when the work breakdown structure, schedule, budget and deliverables are developed.

The advantages of the '80 hour' rule forces the project manager and team to:

- focus fast, and reduces or eliminates scope creep
- get down to details early, and facilitates planning, budgeting and scheduling
- identify incremental deliverables (think product, not process)
- facilitate status reviews, communications and reporting
- overcome project drifting
- identify roles, responsibility and ownership early

Mandatory and discretionary project management key performance indicators

Project management metrics and key performance indicators (KPIs) should be easily captured, as normal output of transaction-based systems within an organization (such as an accounting and/or project management time reporting tracking and purchasing system). The KPIs should communicate the health of a program or project, a task, phase and/or deliverable, and should be determined by each organization in terms of whether it is mandatory or discretionary. The KPIs should also link business objectives to projects as part of IT governance, and should measure progress against a baseline for possible corrective actions. Most organizations will not support, or have difficulty supporting, multiple unsynchronized project data collection and reporting systems that are not an integral part of their operational or financial performance reporting and review processes.

The characteristics of KPIs should be quantifiable, trackable, measurable, comparable and actionable. Each organization must decide which project KPIs are mandatory and which are discretionary. Some suggestions follow for each category:

Suggested mandatory metrics:

- time and schedule
- costs - actual versus budgeted costs
- status of critical path (are we on target based on date?)
- deliverable hit ratio – number of planned versus completed deliverables (schedule)
- top issues – number of open issues should be minimized
- top risks of the project (should always be in focus) – with contingency plans
- customer satisfaction

Suggested discretionary metrics:

- milestone hit ratio – number of planned versus actual milestones achieved on targeted period
- actual versus budgeted resources (number of people)
- number of program/project changes
- % of rework and number of changes requested (including costs of change and rework)
- cost performance index (CPI)
- schedule performance index (SPI)
- earned value – requires a time reporting system in place

5.6 Summary and key take aways

Summary

Critical success factors for achieving program and project management excellence include:

Create the right environment and culture:

- establish the appropriate organizational mindset, culture and environment

- obtain executive sponsorship, commitment and multi-level management buy-in
- obtain customer/other stakeholder/project team commitments and ownership
- success depends on creating a sustainable foundation (eg policy, process, metrics) for managing programs and projects, and integrating results and methodologies into the culture of the organization
- define roles and get the right people involved in every program/project phase
- market and re-enforce (eg training, rewards, mentors, tools, flexible processes) the value and benefits of good project management practices
- adopt a flexible and scalable project management process (phases, templates, repository and tools, and tailor when required) to accommodate different program and project types, based on current and emerging industry best practices

Develop program/project plans (based on a flexible and scalable process):
- define the project's scope, objectives, requirements and deliverables
- establish well-defined phases/tasks, 'go/no go' gates and milestones (break the job down into manageable work packages – '80 hour' rule) with realistic baselines (costs, time, resources and contingencies) based on short term incremental and visible deliverables
- define a responsibility assignment matrix – responsible, inform, consult and/or approve
- establish formal change management and risk management processes

Ensure governance and excellent communications:
- establish a governance, control, reporting and escalation policy and process
- manage expectations of all stakeholders proactively
- identify, measure and track mandatory and discretionary vital signs,

metrics and key issues, and take necessary actions quickly – knock obstacles out of the way
- establish frequent and open communications with stakeholders (both formal and informal review meetings) on a daily, weekly, monthly and quarterly basis, depending on the project's importance and closeness to being implemented
- ensure accurate, timely and meaningful monitoring and progress reporting

Institutionalize a project management policy with flexible and scalable processes
- create project management 'centers of excellence' (eg advocacy center, help desk, education, training, subject matter expert help, process development, project tracking, certification requirements, etc.)
- create a reward and/or recognition policy to re-enforce and sustain
- conduct formal program/project reviews
- develop and use consistent, flexible and scalable project management processes (eg fast track or light versus complex projects) and automate processes and tools (web-based)
- capture and apply lessons learned, and focus on continuous improvement

Key take aways

Project management is a key component of IT governance. Key take aways for effective project management include:
- Executive sponsorship, management buy-in and customer ownership is critical.
- Planning is vital – scope, requirements and schedule
- Project leadership and team building is essential - the team must be empowered to make decisions

- A flexible and scalable process is crucial
- A formal governance and escalation process with meaningful metrics (measurable, traceable, comparable and accurate) with consequential actions is essential
- Effective, frequent, honest and open communications is essential
- Risk management and change management are imperative
- The focus should be on frequent delivery of products
- Decomposing complex projects via WBS (Work Breakdown Structure) into manageable work packages is essential
- Get the right people involved and committed during each phase
- Establish project acceptance criteria between customer and project manager
- Competing on speed is doable and sustainable
- Establish clear and unambiguous accountability (roles and responsibilities)
- Let the business and project dictate the level of project management detail required; however, establish a minimum set of project management processes
- Do project management well and fast (automate as much as possible)
- Make project management an integral part of the corporate and IT governance policy, process and culture
- Provide and mandate project management education and training for all levels of the organization
- Know where you are going, and know when you have got there

Remember, the keys to success are managing the expectations of all constituents and delivering what you promise to maintain credibility; execute as flawlessly as possible and create value for the customer and organization through **flexible discipline**.

Chapter 6
IT Service Management (ITSM) excellence (execution management)

6.1 Overview

This chapter describes the principles and practices of IT Service Management. It provides an overview of ITIL (IT Infrastructure Library) and the eleven process areas and one function, including the relationships of the various processes to each other, as described in version 2 (v2) of ITIL. Specific objectives, benefits and key performance indicators are covered. It also describes the newest version of ITIL – version 3 (v3) 'IT Service Lifecycle', which was released in 2007.

IT Service Management is about maximizing the ability of IT to provide services that are cost effective, and meet or exceed the needs and expectations of the business to:
- reduce the costs of operations
- improve service quality
- improve customer satisfaction
- improve compliance

Figure 6.1 illustrates the benefits of a well executed IT Service Management strategy.

Well executed IT Service Management is about optimizing the ability of IT to provide services that are cost-effective and meet the needs of the business.

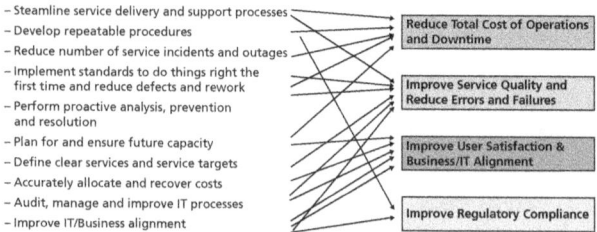

– Steamline service delivery and support processes
– Develop repeatable procedures
– Reduce number of service incidents and outages
– Implement standards to do things right the first time and reduce defects and rework
– Perform proactive analysis, prevention and resolution
– Plan for and ensure future capacity
– Define clear services and service targets
– Accurately allocate and recover costs
– Audit, manage and improve IT processes
– Improve IT/Business alignment

Reduce Total Cost of Operations and Downtime

Improve Service Quality and Reduce Errors and Failures

Improve User Satisfaction & Business/IT Alignment

Improve Regulatory Compliance

Figure 6.1 Benefits map of IT Service Management

6.2 Principles for achieving IT Service Management excellence

Select best practices for achieving superior IT Service Management

Based on a review of best practice companies, a number of consistent practices seem to be prevalent in these organizations regarding superior IT Service Management. They include:

- All steady-state operations (eg PBX, Data Center, Help Desk, Network Management, etc.) must have a primary owner and secondary (backup) owner.
- The overall ITSM budget should be divided into a set of defined products and services, so that all IT costs can be mapped to supportable business processes, either directly or indirectly
- All IT services should consistently achieve the desired level of efficiency, productivity, reliability and availability, as measured by the appropriate key performance indicators (eg service level agreements, customer satisfaction, costs, etc.)

- Most IT services should be described as processes that are well documented, consistently performed and repeatable to maximize their efficiency.
- Most ITSM services should be charged back to the user or customer organization to achieve a greater level of accountability. This requires an established asset management system, a service level management process and a service catalogue.
- The use of an IT service catalogue that can define, price and provide estimated installation time for repetitive productized IT services (install a new computer or network connection) is growing in use, and can benefit the customer by providing an easy way to select, order and communicate to IT the required services desired by the customer. The service catalogue is only partially applied to complex, one time initiatives that are not repetitive
- A formal ITSM governance, reporting and escalation process should be established to resolve key operational issues and risks, and conduct periodic reviews. All steady-state operations have business continuity, back-up (including one or more off-site locations), disaster recovery and security policies and procedures
- All ITSM related processes should be documented in a consistent, repeatable and standard framework, consisting of life cycles, processes and metrics, such as ITIL (IT Infrastructure Library) or ISO/IEC 20000, and continuously improved.
- Optimizing the utilization of IT assets and resources is critical

ITSM standard overview - ISO/ IEC 20000

The standard was originally developed and published in 2000 as BS15000 by a committee of the BSI (British Standards Institution), which comprised of IT service managers from vendor and user groups, including the ITSMF, OGC and others. Version 2 of the standard was developed in 2002. The formal certification scheme for organizations wishing to demonstrate their conformance to the requirements of ISO/ IEC 20000 is currently owned and administered by ITSMF.

ISO/ IEC 20000 applies to IT Service Management users and providers. The standard comprises two parts and both parts share a common structure which includes the following sections:

- scope
- terms and definitions
- requirements for a management system
- planning and implementing Service Management
- planning and implementing new or changed services
- service delivery processes
- relationship processes
- resolution processes
- control processes
- release processes

There are four kinds of process areas that are all related to the fifth process area, the control processes.

The service delivery processes consist of:
- service level management
- service reporting
- service continuity
- availability management
- budgeting and accounting for IT services
- capacity management
- information security management

The relationship processes are:
- business relationship management
- supplier management

The resolution processes are
- incident management
- problem management

The control processes are:
- configuration management
- change management

The release process is defined as a standalone process.

The ISO/ IEC 20000 standard is concerned with IT Service Management and primarily represents a measure of process conformance to be achieved by an organization. In other words, ISO/ IEC 20000 is a corporate standard and its certification applies to organizations, while ITIL focuses on individual certifications.

The relationship between ISO/ IEC 20000 and ITIL is synergistic. The standard addresses the questions relating to IT Service Management as the *'why and what?'* ITIL, on the other hand, complements the standard by addressing the question of *'how?'* and providing the process definitions and other details. Key industry experts have indicated that both ITIL v2 and v3 are consistent with the requirements of ISO/ IEC 20000.

6.3   What is ITIL and why is it different?

Key elements of ITIL (IT Infrastructure Library)

Initiated by CCTA (the UK Government's Central Computing and Telecommunications Agency – now the OGC – Office of Government Commerce), ITIL represents a systematic approach to the management and delivery of quality IT services. ITIL is vendor neutral, flexible and scalable, and focuses on best practices that can be utilized in different ways, depending on the needs and maturity level of organizations. Major elements of ITIL include:

- The ITIL framework provides an effective foundation for higher quality IT Service Management.
- ITIL consists of repeatable, documented best practice life cycle phases, and key processes based on common terminology essential for more effectively managing and improving IT Service Management. It includes checklists, tasks, procedures and responsibilities.
- ITIL aligns with an ISO standard (ISO/ IEC 20000).
- The APM Group (APMG) – In 2006, OGC contracted the management of ITIL rights, the certification of ITIL exams and accreditation criteria to APMG, a commercial organization. APMG defines the certification and accreditation for the ITIL exams, and published the new ITIL version 3 (v3) certification system. In addition, ITIL v3 has been documented as five books. Each book focuses on one of the five phases of the new ITIL v3 IT Service Lifecycle.
- The itSMF (Information Technology Service Management Forum) – was originally established in the UK and the Netherlands in the early 1990s, and has since expanded into over forty-five country chapters, loosely co-ordinated under the umbrella organization, itSMF International (itSMF-I). The organization promotes the IT Service Management profession, and shares information amongst the chapters.

itSMF-I promotes the use of ITIL, ISO/ IEC 20000 and other relevant frameworks.

- EXIN (Dutch) and ISEB (UK) are licensed by OGC; EXIN and ISEB co-operate in the development and provisioning of ITIL v2 and ITIL V3 certifications and other certifications. Both organizations are also contracted by APMG to administer ITIL exams for the ITIL v3 certification.
- Standardized approach and terminology
  - standardization of processes and key performance indicators
  - provides the quality assurance foundation for ISO 9001
  - industry supported software and tools
  - supports Sarbanes-Oxley and other regulations

Advantages of ITIL to customers, constituents and the IT organization

Using ITIL as part of ITSM provides advantages to the customer, business and the IT organization.

Advantages of ITIL to customer and business

- provision of IT services becomes more customer-focused, and agreements about service quality and adherence to SLAs improve the relationship
- the services are described better, in customer language, and in more appropriate detail (as in an IT Service Catalogue)
- the quality and cost of the services are managed better and more effectively.
- communication with the IT organization is improved, by agreeing to limited points of contact
- provides 'cost' visibility to the customer and a better understanding of TCO (Total Cost of Operations)

Advantages of ITIL to the IT organization

- IT organization develops a clearer structure, improves accountability and documentation; it provides a standardized approach to managing and controlling IT
- change, problem and release management is formalized, authorized and traceable; it facilitates the control of increased scale and complexity of the modern IT organization
- facilitates decisions to outsource select services
- encourages the cultural change and migration towards a more effective and more mature organization
- facilitates SOX and other compliance regulations

Potential issues with ITIL

As with all things, where there are advantages, there are also issues or limitations. These include the following:

- Introduction of ITIL is lengthy and represents a significant cost and resource commitment. IT requires prioritization and agreement on key processes, check lists and accountability for implementation and continuous process improvement.
- Improvement in the provision of services and cost reductions are insufficiently visible and poorly communicated to the customer and the business. Immediate ROI cannot always be demonstrated.
- A successful implementation requires the involvement and commitment of personnel at all levels in the organization
- ITIL v2 and v3 do not represent a framework designed as one coherent model, which most organizations would prefer. Rather, it appears to be a continuum of life cycle phases, processes and checklists, which represent a guideline of customizable best practices, rather than a prescriptive approach.

6.4 ITIL frameworks, certifications and qualifications

Background

In 2007, the APMG launched a new certification framework for ITIL, based on ITIL version 3 (v3). ITIL version 2 is to be maintained for a transition period, and is to be continued until 2008.

ITIL v3 represents a major revision to ITIL v2. ITIL v3 approaches IT Service Management from a life cycle perspective, and the way in which the various phases and processes are linked and interrelated. In ITIL v2, there are twelve (12) process components of ITIL, segmented into two major areas, namely service delivery and service support. Some of these processes have been retained in v3, others eliminated or combined, while new ones have been added.

ITIL version 3 Service Lifecycle, processes and related activities

The new IT Service Lifecycle consists of five phases (Office of Government Commerce, 2007). These phases are:

- **Service Strategy** – This phase includes the design, development and implementation planning of Service Management as a strategic resource from a macro-perspective. It also monitors the effect of strategies, standards, policy and design decisions.

- **Service Design** - This phase includes the design phase for IT services, including such areas as architecture, processes, policy, suggested metrics, check lists and other documentation. It includes the major processes of service catalogue management, service level management, capacity management, availability management, IT service continuity management, security management and supplier management.

- **Service Transition** – This phase involves the transition of newly developed or acquired hardware, software, network components or other services from development (or acquisition) to operations or a production environment. One of the first things one notices is that service asset and configuration replaces configuration, and release and deployment management seems to replace release management. There are four new Service Transition processes: transition planning and support, service validation and testing, evaluation and knowledge management (Kuhn, 2007). This seems like a significant improvement over the ITIL v2 processes, and in particular, focuses on several key areas of vulnerability for many organizations that have not done a good job of transitioning work from systems development to operations.

- **Service Operation** – This is the phase of achieving effectiveness and efficiency in providing and supporting services, in order to ensure value for the customer and the service provider. Major processes within Service Operation include: event management, incident management, problem management, request fulfilment, access management and monitoring and control of IT operations.

- **Continual Service Improvement** – the phase of creating and maintaining the value for the customer by design improvement, and service introduction and operation

Figure 6.2 shows the ITIL v3 Service Lifecycle. Figure 6.3 maps the relevant ITIL v3 processes and related activities to each of the Lifecycle phases. Many of the processes are also part of ITIL v2 and will be defined in more detail in this chapter.

ITIL Version 3 consists of five(5) phases – Service Strategy, Service Design, Service Transition, Service Operation and Continual Service Improvement. Each Phase consists of Numerous Processes, Functions and Related Activities.

OGC contracted the management of ITIL rights, the certification of ITIL exams and accreditation to APMG. APMG defines the certification and accreditation for the ITIL exams and published the new ITIL Version 3 (v3) certification system.

ITIL v3 has been documented as five books. Each book focuses on one of the five phases of the new v3 IT Service Lifecycle.

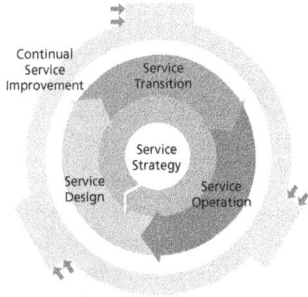

Source: APMG

Figure 6.2 IT Service Management Lifecycle (ITILv3)

Service Strategy	Service Design*	Service Transition*	Service Operation*	Continual Service Improvement

• **Defining the Market**
  – Understand customers
  – Understand opportunity
 	
• Develop Business Case
 	
• Develop the Service Plan
	• Service Catalogue Management (New in v3)
	
	• Service Level Management
	
	• Capacity Management
	
	• Availability Management
	
	• IT Service Continuity Management (ITSCM)
	
	• Information Security Management
	
	• Supplier Management (New in v3)
		• Transition Planning and Support (New in v3)
		
		• Change Management
		
		• Service Asset and Configuration Management** (Revised for v3)
		
		• Release and Deployment Management** (Revised for v3)
		
		• Service Validation and Testing Evaluation (New in v3)
		
		• Service Knowledge Management (New in v3)
		
		• Pilots
			• Event Management (New in v3)
			
			• Incident Management
			
			• Problem Management
			
			• **Request Fulfillment** (Service Desk) (Revised for v3)
			
			• Access Management (New in v3)
			
			• Monitoring and Control IT Operations (New in v3)
				• **Defining Cycle:**
				  – Plan
				  – Do
				  – Check
				  – Act
				
				• Report (Metrics)

*   NOTE: All processes in System Design, Service Transition and Service Operations are the same for v2 and v3, except where it is noted as new for v3.
** Service Asset and Configuration Management, Release and Deployment Management have been transitioned and enhanced from v2 to v3 with additional processes.

Figure 6.3 ITIL v3 Service Lifecycle, related processes and selected activities

ITIL v2 and v3 certification and qualifications

ITIL version 2 has three levels of certification:

- **Foundation Level** - Certificate in IT Service Management
- **Practitioner Level** - Certificate in IT Service Management. There are Practitioner Certificates for various processes or functions from ITIL version 2 (Service Level Management, Capacity Management, etc.) and Practitioner Certificates for clusters of the functions and processes (four clusters: Release & Control, Support & Restore, Agree & Define and Plan & Improve)
- **Manager Level** - Certificate in IT Service Management

For ITIL version 3, a completely new system of qualification was set up. There are four qualification levels:

- **Foundation level** – This level is aimed at basic knowledge of, and insight into, the core principles and processes of ITIL version 3. At this level the qualification remains very similar to the old ITIL version 2 Foundation.
- **Intermediate level**:
  - **Intermediate level 1** – The first middle level is aimed at the Service Lifecycle and is built up around the five core books of ITIL version 3: Service Strategy, Service Design, Service Transition, Service Operation and Continual Service Improvement.
  - **Intermediate level 2** – The second middle level is aimed at capabilities and is built up around four clusters: service portfolio & relationship management, service design & optimization, service monitoring & control and service operation & support.
  - The two middle levels are aimed at an insight into, and application of, the knowledge of ITIL version 3. These levels replace the Practitioner and Manager levels of ITIL version 2.

The ITIL version 3 certification framework has been significantly revised to reflect the service lifecycle approach. The new scheme recognizes the value of existing v2 qualifications and introduces a system that enables an individual to gain credits for both ITIL v2 and v3 courses. The ITIL v3 certification will be based on the following structure which will culminate in the award of the ITIL diploma in IT Service Management.

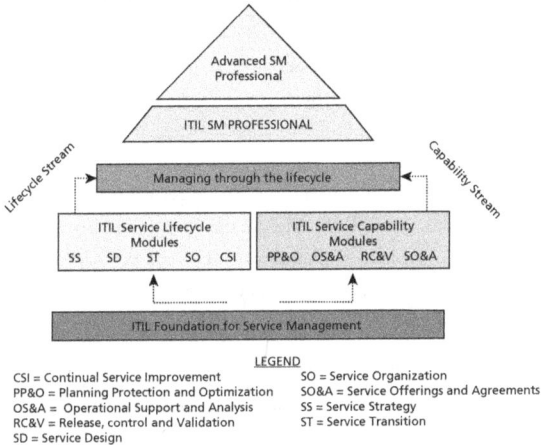

LEGEND

CSI = Continual Service Improvement
PP&O = Planning Protection and Optimization
OS&A = Operational Support and Analysis
RC&V = Release, control and Validation
SD = Service Design

SO = Service Organization
SO&A = Service Offerings and Agreements
SS = Service Strategy
ST = Service Transition

Source: OGC/ APMG

Figure 6.4 ITIL v3 qualifications and certifications

- **Advanced level** – This level was still under development when this book was being written. It is anticipated that this will test the ability to apply ITIL version 3 principles in a real life situation.

For every element in the scheme, a number of credits can be obtained. Credits are also awarded for the certifications from ITIL v2. Various 'bridge exams' are offered in order to connect version 2 certificates to the version 3 exams.

Figure 6.4 presents the new version 3 certification framework and components. The number of credits for each component was not yet finalized when this section was written.

6.5   Major ITIL processes and functions

Summary of ITIL Service Management processes – v2

There are twelve processes and/or functions defined in ITIL v2. Figure
6.5 identifies these processes and segments them into two groupings
– IT service delivery and IT service support. More details of each process
or function is provided below, in terms of definition, key benefits, key
implications from an IT Service Management perspective and select key
performance indicators (KPIs). Most of these processes apply to ITIL v3.
Some of them have been combined with others and expanded in scope,
while others have been renamed, and others still have been created as new
processes.

IT Service Delivery Processes – focus on management control to improve the quality,
   stability, availability, continuity and IT financial management and cost structure.
IT Service Support Processes – focus on operational aspects to detect and correct
   problems, and ensure appropriate change, configuration and release management
   authorization and documentation.

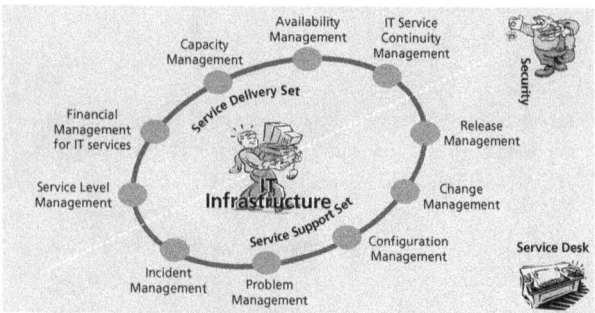

Figure 6.5 ITIL v2 - Service Management processes and functions

For more information on this important Framework please see
Implementing IT Governance as well as other Van Haren titles.

6.6   Steps in making ITIL real and effective

As with other IT governance improvement initiatives, making ITIL real and sustainable requires a number of steps:

- must have corporate mandate from the top
- must have dedicated and available resources
- identify executive champion and multi-disciplinary team
- do your homework, and educate yourself on current and emerging best practices and trends
- conduct an IT Service Management maturity assessment, using a leading best practice process such as CMMI, to assess and define current and target-state base lines for each ITIL process and function; use these baselines to gauge progress and eventually to support implementation success through process improvement
- analyze assessment results and establish a roadmap to achieve a higher level of ITIL maturity
- must recognize that 90% of an ITSM initiative is a 'culture change', and prepare accordingly for a lengthy and involved period of adjustment
- develop and prioritize a program roadmap – process refinement sequence, benefits realization, timetable, and priorities, etc.
- assign an owner to one or more process areas
- encourage and sponsor ITIL certification for key individuals
- develop and conduct a communication and awareness campaign
- establish a 'web Portal' to communicate progress and disseminate information
- plan for and sustain process improvements, and link to a reward and incentive structure; create a 'Continuous Service Improvement' group to sustain the framework
- do not focus on specific ROI as a gauge of success; use TCO (Total Cost of Operation) as a measure of improvement

6.7 Summary and key take aways

Summary

IT Service Management is complex, and requires dedicated resources and leadership to implement effectively. It helps to transition an organization from chaos to order, from a reactive to a proactive environment, from fire fighting (most of the time) to a planned environment (with fire fighting some of the time), and from random service efforts to predictable and more cost effective service quality. An IT Service Management initiative does not end after the framework has been implemented. IT must be continually monitored, maintained and improved. ITIL consists of a repository of five books of best practices that can guide an organization's people, processes and technology towards a common objective of delivering IT service excellence.

ITIL, much as any other IT governance framework, represents a journey that is based on a combination of formal life cycle phases, processes and checklists, combined with common sense and managing change proactively. Each organization can tailor ITIL to fit its environment, culture, resources and level of maturity.

Key take aways

- IT Service Management puts a heavy emphasis on the importance of the Service Lifecycle, and the implementation and improvement of key process areas.
- It is important to identify priorities and critical success factors.
- Processes should be well defined, documented, define organizational interfaces, and be scalable, flexible and measurable.
- Roles and responsibilities should be well defined with respect to each ITSM function and process.

- Leverage tools should support and enable the efficient management of ITSM processes.
- It is important to measure and communicate life cycle and process refinement progress, as well as financial and service improvement benefits.

Chapter 7
Strategic sourcing, outsourcing and vendor management excellence

7.1 Overview

According to James Brian Quinn of Dartmouth College, *"outsourcing is one of the greatest organizational and industry structure shifts of the 21st century"* (Quinn, 2000).

Strategic IT sourcing, outsourcing and vendor management is part of execution management, and, due to its growth, has become a critical component of IT governance. According to a blend of International Data Corporation and Gartner estimates, the IT outsourcing business will exceed $1.0 trillion by 2008-09. This does not include other outsourcing services, such as business process outsourcing, legal, accounting, manufacturing, customer services, medical, administrative services and many others.

Strategic sourcing and outsourcing definitions

According to the International Association of Outsourcing Professionals (IAOP) outsourcing is a long-term, results-oriented business relationship with a specialized third party services provider that can be strategic and transformational or tactical or both (IAOP, May, 2007):

- **Strategic or transformational sourcing** – assets and processes are transferred to service providers and/or core competencies are supplemented by service providers' centers of excellence (eg R & D,

Product Design/Development, etc.). This represents a business focus, and is all about creating value; it aligns with the business processes that change in line with strategic business goals and objectives, and is based on the creation of a 'win-win' partnership between the customer and the service provider.

- **Tactical outsourcing** – can include staff supplementation and easily scalable IT services, such as additional web server or application services provider (ASP) capacity, where there are no asset transfers. These are often linked to specific problems or opportunities in a company with an operational focus, and are all about adding resources or capacity for a limited time period.

Other terms that are associated with outsourcing include:

- **Onshore (Home Country) outsourcing** – obtaining services from an external source in your home country
- **Rural outsourcing** – variation of home country outsourcing, where an organization obtains the services of an external source in a rural area of the home country, where the service is usually less expensive than in an urban part of the country
- **Near - shore outsourcing** – refers to a service provider located in a country which is near to your home country, often one that shares a border. Canada or Mexico are near – shore countries for US-based customers
- **Offshore outsourcing** – refers to contracting with a company that is geographically distant, like India, Ireland, China, Philippines, Israel and Rumania, where an ocean separates the countries
- **Best - shore outsourcing** – a recently coined term that describes the 'shore' that offers the best 'deal' for the customer

In addition to the IAOP, another excellent reference for client and service provider outsourcing best practice frameworks, processes and tools was developed by a consortium led by Carnegie Mellon University's Information Technology Services Qualification Center (ITSqc). ITSqc published two documents, one of which is the eSourcing Capability Model for Service Providers; the other is the eSourcing Capability Model for Client Organizations.

Major outsourcing trends and challenges

There are a number of trends and challenges associated with outsourcing. The outsourcing industry has become global, with India still in the lead in the offshore services area, and other regions and countries becoming much more active in gaining entry in the industry.

Major outsourcing trends and challenges include:

- Market trends in contracting are changing - total contract value and duration is trending lower, based on traditional outsourcing contracts, and is spread across a limited number of preferred service providers by customers.
- Customers are increasingly going with strategic sourcing specialists such as IT, business process outsourcing, human resources, finance and accounting.
- Business process and knowledge management outsourcing is growing faster than IT.
- Customers are placing increased pressure on service providers to be certified or licensed (eg ISO 9000, SEI's CMMI, PMI's PMP, ITIL, CPA, ISO 17799, CSSP, etc.).

- Outsourcing can be challenging - according to a Deloitte Consulting Survey of 25 large companies, 70% have had negative experiences and have brought some outsourcing work back in-house, for the following reasons (Deloitte, December, 2005):
  - improved quality/management by in-sourcing – 65%
  - functions being outsourced became strategic/core – 44%
  - increased cost savings by in-sourcing – 33%
  - vendor inflexibility – 11%
- Additional lessons from the study included the trend that firms tend to switch from being cost-focused to being growth-focused as the economy grows, and outsourcing is increasingly becoming an issue of business strategy. Alternatives that must be evaluated are not only cost reduction benefits, but also improved innovation techniques.
- According to a recent Forrester Research report on outsourcing with over 100 organizations:
  - 53% reported that they have outsourcing challenges because their companies lacked or were weak in project management skills and competencies for managing outsourcing work
  - 58% reported that they lacked a good process for specifying the work
  - 48% said they did not have the right metrics for measuring adequate service provider performance metrics

Why do organizations outsource?

There are many reasons why organizations choose to outsource or in-source, or deploy a combination of both strategies. Figure 7.1 provides a list of outsourcing (or buy) and in-sourcing (or build) motivations.

BUY (OUTSOURCING) CRITERIA	BUILD (IN-SOURCING) CRITERIA
Cost Reduction	Competitive advantage (proprietary requirements)
Speed up time-to-market	Expertise available in-house
Assist a rapid growth situation or overflow situations	May be less expensive than buying
Aggressive Schedule	Can be completed on time
Politically correct	Opportunity costs trade-offs
Lower risk	No suitable vendors available
Improve flexibility	Core competency
Acquire new skills/resources/management	Security and control are critical
Avoid major capital investments	Strategic initiative or function or process
Improve performance	Threat to intellectual property theft
Enable innovation	

Figure 7.1 Sourcing motivations – build versus buy

What do organizations outsource?

Today, virtually any IT functions can be outsourced such as:

- **IT architecture** – includes database management, data architecture, etc.
- **IT infrastructure** – elements of the IT infrastructure include computer center, network management and operations, help desk operations, data entry, hardware maintenance and service, etc.
- **Systems and software development and maintenance** – coding, testing, integration, maintenance, etc.
- **Web development and hosting** – e-commerce front end, middleware and backend systems
- **Training, education and certification** – IT, customer and management personnel

Examples of recent IT and other outsourcing deals demonstrate the extent to which select companies outsource both core functions and non-core functions or processes:

- Brokerage firm – outsourced data center and network operations
- Computer manufacturer – outsourced assembly of its PCs and call center
- Medical office – outsourced transcription of doctor's voice recording notes on a patient off-shore
- Bank – outsourced customer service center and IT help desk
- Pharmaceutical company – outsourced manufacture of product
- University – hired a service provider to manage its entire IT function and transferred all IT assets to the service provider
- Architecture firm – outsourced design and blueprints of buildings to eastern Europe
- Airplane manufacturer – outsourced the manufacture of different components to strategic partner vendors in different countries with large market potential
- Retail firm – outsourced their payroll and select accounting functions
- Consulting firm – outsourced the design, development and maintenance of their website
- Law firm – experimenting with outsourcing legal research off-shore for US clients

All of the above demonstrate the way in which we now operate in a global economy, and doing business in developing and emerging countries is part of the model. It is always useful to start with a business model evaluation of the outsourcing opportunity, and then an assessment of what is core and non-core to IT, and what can be supplemented by global service provider resources. As an example, a large telecommunications company uses offshore locations in India and Brazil to promote a 'follow-the-sun-model' for IT testing and production support.

Benefits of outsourcing from a customer and service provider perspective

There are many benefits to outsourcing from a customer's perspective. They include:

- enables business to focus on strategic functions
- lowers annual operating costs and capital investments
- frees up time and resources (opportunity costs) to focus on core strengths
- increases speed to market
- provides access to scarce or supplementary resources
- capital infusion (depending on what is outsourced) for assets that are transferred
- more politically acceptable in certain situations, if the in-house function does not have a good reputation
- provides scalable resources and bench strength
- enables greater innovation
- improves productivity and quality through individual or company certifications

There are also benefits and market realities from a service provider perspective, such as:

- substantial revenue stream potential and growing global market
- long-term customer relationships, with opportunities for cross-selling and up-selling other products and services
- Increasingly, customers are going with a limited number strategic sourcing specialist to develop longer term relationships and negotiate better deals

Barriers to and risks of outsourcing

While there are many good reasons to outsource, there are also barriers and risks that need to be overcome or mitigated, especially in dealing with off-shore deals. Select obstacles and risks are:

- loss of control of confidential information
- function or process is too critical to outsource
- loss of flexibility due to inflexible contracts
- negative customer reaction
- employee resistance due to job loss or transfer
- poor outsourcing process or management
- service provider failure
- lack of intellectual property protection
- differences in culture and time zones relating to offshore deals
- regulatory and legal country differences
- lack of security and data protection
- legal and arbitration adjudication and dispute settlement
- off-shore bribery

7.2   Principles and practices for outsourcing excellence from a customer perspective

Even with the increased outsourcing initiatives in customer organizations, it appears that organizations continue to struggle with establishing and enforcing a more formal, consistent and repeatable outsourcing policy, process and methodology.

According to the ITsqc at Carnegie Mellon University, *"managing and meeting client expectations is a major challenge for service providers in these business relationships, and examples of failures abound"* (Hefley and Locsche, 2006).

They go on to summarize the key issues faced by customer organizations, which are also re-enforced and supplemented by the IAOP in their outsourcing body of knowledge (IAOP, 2006):

- establishing an appropriate outsourcing strategy, business case and plan
- identifying the appropriate outsourcing opportunities
- developing appropriate approaches and techniques for outsourcing activities
- identifying, selecting and negotiating 'win-win' deal service providers
- managing service provider governance and performance management
- managing the transition from the customer to the service provider as a project
- managing the on-going relationship

Based on an extensive review of the literature and select case studies, there are a number of best practice principles and practices that can represent a checklist, for helping companies achieve improvements and higher levels of outsourcing maturity and effectiveness in their environments.

Key principles and practices for outsourcing excellence

General:
- have a clear strategy and plan that supports the business:
  - what are you expecting to achieve and what would success look like?
  - at what cost?
- the clarity of purpose for both sides with defined roles and responsibilities
- establish key performance measures that are realistic and meaningful
- empowerment - let people do what they are suppose to do – hold them accountable, both on the service provider and customer side
- have an escalation policy and process, with clear roles and responsibilities for both sides

- periodic, formal progress reviews and reports, based on specific metrics relating to the type of outsourcing service or project
- for large initiatives, establish a high level peer outsourcing governance board for joint reviews
- assign a service provider account relationship manager as a single point of contact/interface with the customer, and establish a customer/service provider relationship model
- keep closer tabs on the relationship during first 90 days of a contract, and make any necessary adjustments fast

Customer 'to do's':
Key customer 'to do's' should include:

- executive alignment and commitment to outsourcing that creates a favorable outsourcing culture within the organization
- create a well defined and realistic business case process and case
- establish a consistent and formal process for service provider selection and contract negotiations
- develop an outsourcing transition plan from pilot to full implementation provision, for either re-deployment or termination of displaced resources
- build key performance indicators into the contract performance evaluation system, with both rewards for extra-ordinary performance and penalties for poor performance
- make KPIs relevant, simple, comparable, easy to report and focused on measurable outcomes
- develop an outsourcing communication plan, risk management and mitigation plan, policy and process
- balance stakeholder needs – companies that successfully outsource continuously 'take the pulse' of all stakeholder groups, to adjust their needs over time

- pursue stakeholder involvement on major outsourcing deals through governance boards, steering committees and working committees
- manage the expectations of all stakeholders well – deliver what you promise; do not over-promise things you or the outsourcing service provider cannot deliver – credibility is a fleeting attribute that if lost, is extremely difficult or almost impossible to regain
- experience matters – governance groups can rapidly fill their experience deficit through subject matter expert coaching or outside consulting support
- SLAs are not enough – service-level agreements are extremely important and should be continuously refined and improved over the life of the contract; however, they must be augmented by other methods to ensure customer satisfaction (eg formal and/or informal surveys, listening to the voice of the customer, etc.)
- develop disengagement options and conditions as part of the contract that includes renegotiations options
- make sure that a disaster prevention and recovery plan with contingencies is in place

Avoiding the major sins of outsourcing

For every 'do', there is a 'don't'. These include the following:

- lack of executive management commitment
- lack of an outsourcing communications plan
- minimum knowledge of outsourcing processes and techniques
- failure to recognize outsourcing risks
- failure to obtain assistance from outside outsourcing experts and professionals
- not dedicating the best and brightest internal resources
- rushing through the outsourcing requirements, scope, RFP and vendor selection and contract phases

- not recognizing the impact of cultural differences
- underestimating what it will take to get the vendor to become productive
- no formal outsourcing governance program
- do not put all of your eggs in one service provider's basket; split the work or designate a primary and secondary service provider for back-up purposes
- do not de-skill by outsourcing all of an organizations knowledge and experience in particular areas, so that one becomes overly or dangerously dependent on the service provider

Customer's outsourcing planning checklist

It is always useful to have a checklist as a reminder of the activities that should be considered. The following provides such a checklist for outsourcing:

- executive sponsor (s)
- charter define boundaries
- appoint an outsourcing project team and manager – pre – outsourcing stage and post-outsourcing stage (if outsourcing is pursued)
- project scope and requirements
- assumptions, obstacles and constraints
- core and non-core competencies
- critical success factors
- business case (cost/benefit analysis, including impact on current employees and unions, where applicable)
- communications plan
- work breakdown structure
- roles and responsibilities – customer and service provider
- resource plan

- risk management and contingency plan
- procurement and contracting plan
- service provider selection and evaluation criteria, with a consistent weighting scheme
- quality plan
- governance plan, escalation and key metrics
- project or service schedule and deliverables
- change management plan
- implementation, conversion and transition plan
- disengagement plan
- develop a list of qualified service providers for consideration

Outsourcing life cycle

Outsourcing initiatives, like projects, have life cycles with phases or stages or both. The following examples are provided by the IAOP and the ITesq respectively.

Stages of outsourcing life cycle and 'go/go no' criteria

As part of their Outsourcing Professional Body of Knowledge (OPBOK®), the IAOP has defined five stages of outsourcing as follows (IAOP, 2006):

- **Idea stage** - which outsourcing opportunities are appropriate in support of the organization's business strategy?
- **Assessment and planning stage** - with the development of the business case and of the provider marketplace, are the anticipated benefits, indeed, real?
- **Implementation stage** - can we reach agreement on a deal with one or more of the service providers?
- **Transition stage** - can we execute successfully?

- **Management (operating) stage** - with the transition complete, are
  we ready to operate under the new agreement? Are the benefits being
  realized?

Figure 7.2 illustrates the five stages.

**The five stages of outsourcing include: idea, assessment and planning,
implementation, transitions and management (ongoing).**

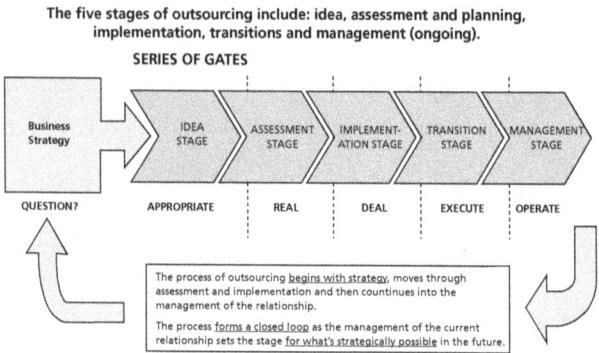

Source: IAOP

Figure 7.2 Five stages of outsourcing

Figure 7.3 summarizes the key deliverable and 'go/no' go criteria, by
outsourcing stage.

Sourcing life cycle

Another outsourcing life cycle alternative has been developed and
documented by the ITesq. A summary of the life cycle phases include:

- **On-going management phase** - spans the entire outsourcing life cycle
- **Initiation phase** – includes business case, vendor selection, negotiation,
  contracting and deployment planning

Stage	Idea	Assessment & Planning	Implementation	Transition	Management
Deliverables	• Develop Concept • Perform High Level Review of Operations • Identify corporate direction • Perform Situation Analysis & identify Outsourcing Opportunity • Get executive sponsor • Assign Steering Comm.	• Analyze current processes & functions • **Define proposed processes & functions** • **Define user needs** • Perform risk analysis • Develop business case (with plan)	• Issue RFP • Finalize deal structure and terms • Develop and negotiate contract • Develop human resource and asset transfer plan • Communications Plan • Governance plan	• Detailed transition plan (with pilot) • Implement new organization structure • Transfer people, assets, functions and/or processes • Develop training plan • Outplacement plan and arrangements of personnel	• Perform daily management activities • Monitor performance • Implement relationship management process • Institute change management process
Go/No Go Criteria	Appropriate? • Alignment with business strategy? • Core competency? • High level **cost/benefit** acceptable? • Acceptable risk? • Competitive advantage? • Legal, ethical, etc.?	Real? • Acceptable business case? • Acceptable risk? • Acceptable reward/ risk analysis?	Deal? • Approved/ signed contract?	Execute? • Approved transition plan? • Approved pilot? • Monitor progress during transition **and fix issues as necessary** • **Defined roles and responsibilities for all transition tasks**	Operate? • Governance and Metrics Being Met? • Renew, Expand, or Disengage?

Figure 7.3 Key deliverables and 'go/no go' decision criteria by outsourcing stage

- **Delivery phase** - involves the transition to the service provider or provision of the service provider's deliverables
- **Completion phase** – extends the contract or re-insources the functions, processes or services

7.3 Vendor selection, contract negotiations and governance process

Steps in vendor selection and RFIs, RFQs and RFPs

There are a number of steps that, if followed will facilitate the vendor selection and negotiations process. These assume that an outsourcing business case has been completed and approved.

- convene the project manager and vendor selection team
- identify appropriate and qualified vendors

- set a realistic schedule
- define vendor evaluation criteria and weights before issuing bid requests (to maintain objectivity)
- prepare requests for proposal (RFPs); if necessary or desired, an RFI and an RFQ
- evaluate the bids
- conduct a due diligence investigation on the most likely service provider(s) to be selected; visit the vendor locations and interview the people who will be doing the work
- negotiate the deal
- select a vendor
- sign the contract

Figure 7.4 identifies the vendor selection, evaluation, contract negotiations and award process flow.

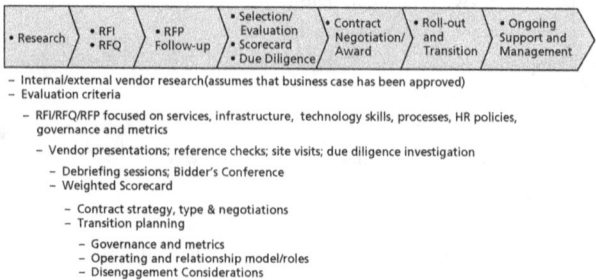

- Internal/external vendor research(assumes that business case has been approved)
- Evaluation criteria

  - RFI/RFQ/RFP focused on services, infrastructure, technology skills, processes, HR policies, governance and metrics

    - Vendor presentations; reference checks; site visits; due diligence investigation

      - Debriefing sessions; Bidder's Conference
      - Weighted Scorecard

        - Contract strategy, type & negotiations
        - Transition planning

          - Governance and metrics
          - Operating and relationship model/roles
          - Disengagement Considerations

Figure 7.4 Vendor selection, evaluation, contract negotiations and award process flow

Vendor evaluation criteria and weights

While companies may use different criteria, and assign different weights for selection criteria, it is nevertheless important that within a given organization, the criteria and weights are consistently applied on a basis which is as objective as possible. Figure 7.5 lists a number of vendor evaluation criteria, organized by four major weighted categories, including demonstrated competencies, total capabilities, fit and competitiveness of solution and relationship fit and dynamics.

Demonstrated Competencies – 20% (Weight)	Competitiveness of Solution – 40%
– People (Recruitment, Training, Experience)	– Solution itself (Fit to Requirements, Innovative)
– **Processes (Benchmarking, Certification, Continuous Improvement)**	– Service Delivery (Quality of Processes/Tools/ Resources, Performance, Management Depth and Capabilities)
– Technologies (Level of Investment, Leading Edge)	– Risks and Risk Sharing
– Experience (Functional, Industry)	– Financial Proposal (Pricing, Volume Considerations, Structure, Switching Costs)
– **Proven Performance & Certifications**	– Terms and Conditions (Commercial, Change, Dispute, Adjudication)
– Track Record of Innovation	– Human Resources Requirements (Employee Transition, Career Opportunities)
Vendor Capabilities – 10%	*Relationship Dynamics – 30%*
– Financial Strength and Stability	– *Culture*
– Infrastructure and Resources (Bench Strength, Weaknesses/Points of Failure)	– *Mission and Strategy*
– Management Systems	– *Relationship Management (Flexibility, Partnership, Trust, Executive Presence, Governance and Reporting)*
– Complete Suite of Services (Type and Scope, Ability to Scale, Backup, Redundancy, Security, IP protection, etc.)	– *Relative Importance (Size, as a Client)*
	– *Achievement (esp. existing relationship)*

Source: IAOP; Weights for each evaluation component will vary by organization.

Figure 7.5 Scoring and selecting potential vendors

Outsourcing governance process, organization, escalation and metrics

Some best practice starting points for measuring outsourcing performance include:

- clarify objectives at the start of the negotiations to align for success
- choose fewer metrics with higher stakes (and increase the rewards and penalties accordingly) in order to help focus, minimize administrative demands and improve the relationship
- shift from input to output metrics, where possible; instead of counting

how many hours it took to complete each order, a photographic firm asked its outsourcer to count how many orders it completed each hour – this helped to speed up the number of orders processed per hour

- define metrics early in the relationship (as part of the contract, not after the contract is signed)
- you get what you pay for; if you demand rock-bottom pricing, do not expect a world-class SLAs

The IT Services Qualification Center (ITSqc) at Carnegie Mellon University suggests the following seven best practices for sourcing governance (ITSqc, 2006):

- **Sourcing policy** – establish and implement the organizational sourcing policy (eg purpose, organization, decision authority, support systems, processes, performance management guidelines, etc.)
- **Service provider management** – establish and implement procedures to manage service providers (eg relationship management, tracking performance, create issues, dispute and escalation process, etc.)
- **Internal stakeholder management** – establish and implement procedures to manage internal stakeholders (eg relationship model, identify liaison personnel, define communications mechanisms, track stakeholder issues and resolutions, etc.)
- **Defined sourcing process** – establish and maintain documented sourcing processes for use across the organization (eg establish sourcing process guidelines and owners of each process, determine measures to track sourcing process performance, etc.)
- **Align strategy and architectures** – align strategies and architectures to support sourcing across the organization (develop and support processes for aligning business strategies and plans with architecture strategy, align IT capability with sourced services, ensure that the business processes performed as sourced services are consistent with, and integrated with, the business processes of the organization, etc.)

- **Business process integration** – establish and implement procedures to manage the integration of business processes with those performed by service providers (eg document and support procedures and processes that enable integration, identify performance measures of the integrated business process, track status, etc.)
- **Adapt to business change** – establish and implement guidelines for reviewing and adapting to changes (eg create change management system and process, for reviewing and adapting to change, create change management and service modification requests for approved changes, etc.).

7.4   Summary steps and key take aways

Summary

Figure 7.6 provides a summary checklist for developing and managing successful outsourcing deals.

As an example, the CIO of a major global telecommunications company suggested the following simple and pragmatic model that works within the environment:

- keep it simple: limit number of vendors on-shore or off-shore
- know who is off-shoring and to what other subs in what other off-shoring countries
- train all levels of the IT organization - managers need to mange globally, not just locally (in-sourced and outsourced functions)
- expect to spend time in the air; visit, visit and visit at multiple levels
- put your IT managers in India, Brazil and China (get on the ground)
- plan for turn-over (not just cheap labor)
- constantly revisit business cases and keep contracts alive
- grow beyond vendors (look at having your own presence in the countries – maximize effectiveness such as with captive subsidiaries)

• Develop a Plan and Build a Business Case
  – Baseline model
  – Requirements & scope
  – Costs (realistic)/savings
  – Contingency Plan
  – Assumptions/Constraint
  – Obstacles
  – Metrics – OLAs, SLAs, Cost, Schedule, Other
 	
• Go/No-Go
  – Communicate decision to stakeholders
 	
• RFP
  – Preparation
  – **Narrow the field - RFI, RFQ**
  – Invitation to Vendors
  – **Vendor briefings**
  – Site visits
  – Vendor proposals
 	
• Evaluation & Selection
  – Multidisciplinary team
  – Qualitative & quantitative evaluation
  – criteria
  – Cultural match/bench strength
  – Due Diligence
  – Final selection
	• Contract Negotiation/Signing
	  – It takes two to tango
	  – Contract types
	    – **Fixed price (well defined)**
	    – **Time & material (not well defined)**
	    – **Cost & fixed fee**
	    – Cost & variable fee
	    – Unit price contract
	  – Terms & Conditions
	  – Change and Risk Management
	  – Governance, Metrics and Escalation
	  – Contingency and Disaster Recovery Options
	  – Disengagement Options & Responsibilities
	    – Triggers and Conditions
	    – Ownership
	    – Transition Roles/Responsibilities
	
	• Transition Management, Contract Management &
	  Performance Monitoring
	    – Transition Planning, Roles, Pilot, Training &
	      Readiness Validation
	    – Assure compliance with project or service
	      objectives, scope, schedule, & deliverables
	    – Measure and evaluate delivered work
	    – Vendor governance and reporting
	    – Integrate vendor tasks and deliverables into
	      Project Plan
	    – Assign Senior Manager/Director/VP to
	      manage vendor relationship with "clout"

Figure 7.6 Summary checklist for managing successful outsourcing deals

Steps in making outsourcing real

The following steps will help to make outsourcing deals real:

- identify executive champion and multi-disciplinary team
- do your homework – educate yourself on current and emerging best practices
- understand current state of organization's level of outsourcing maturity and gaps
- use a formal procurement process with Requests for Information (RFIs), Requests for Quote (RFQs) and Requests for Proposal (RFPs)
- determine the critical factors to be used for service provider selection and evaluation

- negotiate a fair contract for both parties
- develop a transition plan with clear roles and responsibilities
- appoint a senior manager accountable for the results:
  - manage relationship
  - manage contract
  - manage governance, risk and issues escalation
- monitor key performance indicators and resolve issues quickly on a regular basis
- treat the outsourcing work package as part of your company's IT services or projects, and manage the work accordingly

Key take aways

- executive sponsorship is critical
- get the right people involved in each stage
- know your current baseline and costs
- issue an RFP - contract with a primary and secondary vendor (do not put all of your eggs in one basket)
- strong relationship management - create a customer/vendor team and engagement model, with clearly defined roles and responsibilities
- communicate, communicate, communicate
- identify and measure meaningful performance metrics
- short- versus long-term contracts, with more frequent renewable periods
- vendor certification is better than no certification
- manage the vendor - do not let the vendor manage you

Make your peace with sourcing now. Either get on the sourcing train or get in front of it.

Chapter 8
Performance management, management controls and enabling technology excellence

8.1   Overview

As IT investments grow and become a larger share of an enterprise's capital expenditures, IT executives are being required by business executives to demonstrate the business value and alignment of their investments, as well as the reliability, availability, security, continuity and integrity of the information and supporting services. The IT performance management, control and reporting challenge is:

- to communicate from IT outwardly to management and the user community at multiple levels (eg strategic, management, knowledge and operational) and to multiple audiences (eg Board and/or executive management, middle management, knowledge)
- to inwardly direct and manage the IT organization

A performance management, control, continuity and compliance plan must be developed for IT, as part of a governance initiative. The development of the plan should be a collaborative effort between the business and IT. It should be based on a number of objectives, such as strategic, financials, quality, operational and service effectiveness, which support an organization's business vision, mission, plans, objectives and financials.

There are many issues involved in measuring, monitoring and controlling IT that need to be addressed in a comprehensive manner:

- What industry frameworks would be helpful in this area?
- Who should own measurement? Control? Continuity of Service? Compliance?
- What key performance indicators should be measured?
  - business impact – revenues, costs, profits
  - workload, availability, capacity, reliability, scalability
  - agility and speed
  - alignment
  - rate of technology absorption
  - organization fluidity and synergy
  - process innovation (internal and external)
  - program/project management effectiveness
  - service levels
  - integration
  - quality
  - investment impact
  - customer relationship
  - value chain impact
  - historic or predictive or a hybrid of both factors
- What to do with the measurements?
  - establish a report card for performance
  - link each measure to a critical success factor, for the business or for IT, or for both
  - create meaningful, understandable, relevant benchmarks
  - create a set of metrics outwardly bound from IT to the organization
  - create a set of metrics that are inwardly bound to help manage the IT organization
- When should measurements be done? Continuously? Daily? Weekly? Monthly? Quarterly? Semi-annually? Annually?
- What level of measurement detail should be reported and in what reporting format? To whom?

8.2 Principles for achieving performance management and control excellence

As part of improving IT governance, it is critical for an organization to establish an overall framework that includes (amongst other things) an IT enterprise strategy (which includes business capability roadmaps and Balanced Scorecard metrics), performance management, management controls and compliance components. Figure 8.1 represents such a framework for a major communications company. It is interesting to note the highlighted areas, since they specifically focus on IT strategy, compliance, life cycle and reporting.

In addition, by using industry best practice frameworks or guidelines, and their components (such as domains and checklists, such as COSO® and CobiT®), a company can develop a more consistent and sustainable

**Key Components for Performance Management, Compliance and Reporting Include:
IT Enterprise Strategy, Enterprise Compliance, Lifecycle and Quality and Organizational Reporting**

IT Enterprise Strategy
• Balanced Scorecard Metrics
• Business Capability Roadmaps

Organizational Reporting
• Supplier Management
• Ops Reviews & Scorecard Rpts

Enterprise Architecture
• Arch & Technology Roadmaps
• Arch standards and governance

Lifecycle & Quality
• IT methodology & tools
• Project management

Governance

Technology R&D

Pipeline Management
• Supplier scheduling
• Resource management

Enterprise Compliance
• Sarbanes Oxley
• Privacy
• Continuity/Disaster Recovery

Enterprise Applications
• Data Warehouse / Management
• Business Intelligence

Figure 8.1 IT governance – How it works: major communications company

approach to making IT performance management and management
controls more effective and sustainable. Of course, one needs to assign
decision authority, ownership and link deliverables and performance to a
reward structure, to make individuals and teams more accountable. Figure
8.2 illustrates a high level framework, linking COSO® and CoBiT® with
Sarbanes-Oxley (SOX) and the Balanced Scorecard. Organizations that
are not impacted by SOX can substitute whatever compliance regulations
impact their environments.

**A well-designed framework based on industry standards and guidelines can help create
more consistency for performance and compliance management and controls.**

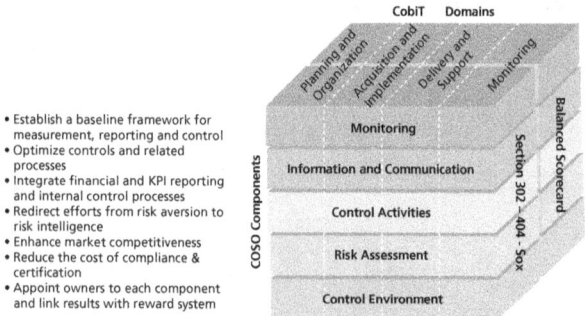

Figure 8.2 A framework for IT governance performance management, management controls
and compliance

Other principles for achieving performance management and management
control excellence include:

- identify critical success factors for the business and IT, and identify the
  key performance indicators (KPIs) linked to these factors
- build key performance indicators into your performance evaluation
  system, starting at the top and permeating to all positions that can
  influence those KPIs

- make KPIs relevant, simple, comparable, easy-to-report and focused on goals and objectives
- define and issue a management control policy and related procedures, which identify all of the areas requiring management controls, using CobiT as a checklist
- monitor, audit and assure that IT operates in accordance with the approved controls
- develop a risk management and mitigation plan, policy and process
- develop a business/IT continuity and disaster recovery plan and policy
- develop a clear performance review, escalation and issues resolution policy and process, with clear accountability and responsibilities

What critical success factors and key performance indicators should be tracked?

IT performance measures have evolved over time. Gartner and others have identified a number of limitations to current IT measurement systems and metrics such as:

- output measures do not tell one how to improve
- historic metrics do not identify issues driving current performance
- there is usually a lack of balance between leading or predictive metrics and lagging or historic metrics; there are usually many more lagging than leading indicators
- many systems reflect a lack of external comparison against best practice organizations
- it is often difficult to measure strategic or added value
- too many metrics; a surplus of metrics overwhelms the scorecard reader and leads to suboptimal use of senior decision-makers' limited time
- no individual impact; the absence of incentives, linking individual behavior to IT Balanced Scorecard use, hampers scorecard application and achievement of targets

The execution of these plans and objectives must be monitored and measured by a combination of Balanced Scorecard key performance indicators (KPIs) as well as formal and informal status review meetings and reports (eg report cards, dashboards). The outcomes should link critical success factors to KPIs that are measurable, part of a standard reporting system and linked to a governance component. If one cannot measure it, it does not count. Remember, one gets what one measures, so it is critical to measure and control the right things.

The Balanced Scorecard system, developed by Drs. Kaplan and Norton, is a management system that provides a clear prescription as to what companies should 'measure' to clarify their vision and strategy, and translate them into actions with respect to four areas: financial, customers, internal business processes and learning and growth.

Figure 8.3 illustrates the original Balanced Scorecard concept for business. Figure 8.4 identifies critical success factors, based on expanded Balanced Scorecard categories, and relates them to key performance indicators, as well as describing key historic and predictive performance metric attributes that are useful for IT.

Each company must tailor the CSFs (critical success factors) and KPIs (key performance indicators) of the Balanced Scorecard to its business strategies, plans and objectives. Each company must also construct a performance report card that should have two audiences – business and IT. One part should focus on key KPIs that are business-centric and are used to communicate from IT outwardly to management and the user community. These include the need for IT to link IT strategy with the business strategy, to monitor service levels, while reducing the TCO (total cost of operations), and to better illustrate the business value of IT. The second part should be IT-centric and should be used by the CIO inwardly to direct, manage and control the performance of the IT organization in

**Identifies what companies should measure to translate
their vision and strategy into actions.**

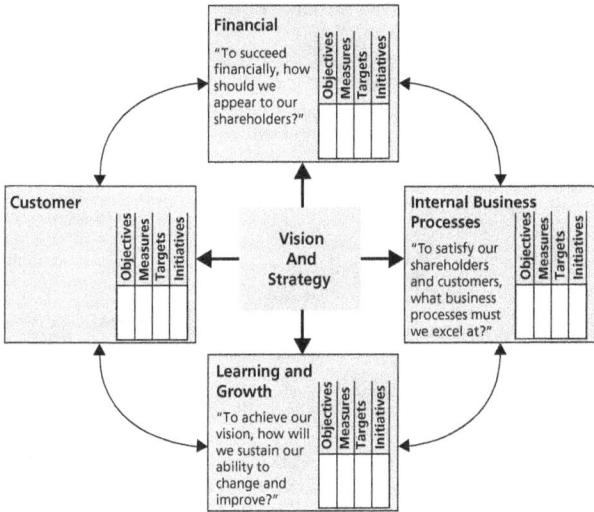

Source: www.balancescorecard.org/basics/bsc1

Figure 8.3 The Balanced Scorecard

terms of customer satisfaction, human capital management, outsourcing
vendor management, resource allocations, project management and Service
Management and delivery.

For one global communications organization, the IT Balanced Scorecard:

- supports the enterprise Balanced Scorecard
- aligns with IT customers' Balanced Scorecards
- cascades down to IT VP level Scorecards
- is directly tied to individual performance objectives

What Key Performance Indicators Should Be Tracked for IT?
The CSFs and KPIs are best determined by the current environment, objectives and strategies of an organization. They must be measurable, comparable & reportable.

- **Critical Success Factor (CSFs) Categories:**
  - Financial*
  - Customer*
  - Employee
  - Process & Product Innovation*
  - Program/Project Innovation
  - Service Level Innovation
  - Learning and Growth*
  - * Balanced Scorecard

- **Key Performance Indicators (KPIs):**
  - Financial
  - Customer – Internal & External
  - Performance – Team & Individual
  - Program/Project Mgt.
  - Skills/Competencies
  - Service availability & readiness

- **Attributes:**
  - Performance (Historic)
    - Time
    - Cost – Reduction, Containment & Avoidance
    - **Profitability – Direct or** Indirect
    - Responsiveness
    - Quality
    - Availability
    - Capacity
    - Reliability
  - Predictive (Future)
    - Maturity Level
    - Capability/Skills
    - Alignment
    - Key Issues
    - Major Risks
    - Customer Satisfaction

Reality Check – Do the CSFs and KPIs...
- Translate into specific actions?
- Help align business and IT?
- Provide leverage to institute change?
- Manage end-to-end results across silos?
- Drive performance and process improvements?
- Allow for benchmarking to compare best practice performance?
- Enhance your ability to compete in the future?
- Drive learning and innovation?
- Predictors of Future Poor Performance?

Figure 8.4 CSFs, KPIs and their key attributes related to IT

The same organization monitors performance against strategy, for each major objective that is identified in the IT plan, and for each objective it also identifies its owner, the metrics used to measure results, specific targets, reports the status of each objective on a monthly basis, and identifies any actions required. On a quarterly basis, an overall IT performance report card is issued to management. The focus includes alignment, major program/project investment management, key IT Service Management and delivery metrics, financial analysis of contributions and expenses, and asset utilization.

Figure 8.5 provides a series of composite Balanced Scorecard metrics, collected from both case study organizations and secondary research, and decomposed into performance metrics covering financial, project management, IT Service Management and vendor performance, IT human resources and customers.

Based on a review of best practice case study companies, using some form of Balanced Scorecard for IT, several critical success factors are necessary to successfully institutionalize IT Balanced Scorecards in organizations:

- make key performance indicators simple, intuitively obvious and focused on goals
- develop key performance indicators with balance and the 'big picture' in mind (outward from IT to the business and inward to manage IT)
- integrate key performance indicators into individual and team performance evaluation systems
- broad executive commitment – use a mix of business and IT leadership in the design, selection, review and continuous improvement of metrics
- develop standard metrics definition based on consensus

8.3   CoBiT® and key management controls

CoBiT® is a model for control of the IT environment. CoBiT stands for Control Objectives for Information and related Technology. CoBiT is a model designed to control and help audit the IT function. This model was originally developed by the Information Systems Audit and Control Foundation (ISACF), the research institute for the Information Systems Audit and Control Association (ISACA). CoBiT was transferred to the IT Governance Institute (ITGI), which is an independent body within ISACA. CoBiT is primarily intended for management, business users of IT and auditors.

Figure 8.6 illustrates the CoBiT framework, its four domains (eg Plan and Organize, Acquire and Implement, Deliver and Support and Monitor and Evaluate) and the IT processes (and controls) that are part of each of the domains.

Financial Performance	
Most Common Metrics	**IT Departmental Cost**
Total IT expenditures as a % of sales	IT cost per employee
IT cost per employee	Total IT spending by geography
Total IT spending by geography	Total IT spending by business unit
% of IT expenditures on new versus maintenance systems	Expenses compared to revenue per quarter
% of "lights on" operating costs (including break/fix, depreciation) versus total IT spend	Spend per portfolio category (e.g. new revenue generation, cost reduction, business transformation)
Project and Investment Cost Performance	Performance against IT spending performance
% of R&D investment resulting in operational applications	Central IT spend as percentage of total IT spend
Total value creation from IT enabled projects	Net present value delivered during payback period
IT Project ROI	
% of key projects completed on time within budget	
IT Service Management and Delivery Costs	
Dollar value of technology assets still in use beyond depreciation schedule	
Share of discretionary spending shared by IT	
% reduction in maintenance cost of all systems	
Average network circuit cost reduction per quarter	
PC/laptop software maintenance cost per month per user	
Workstation software maintenance cost per month per workstation	
E-mail service: cost per month per user	
Infrastructure spending as a % of total IT spending	
Total maintenance cost	
% of year-over-year cost reduction per service	
Total cost of ownership of IT services versus external benchmarks	
Service unit cost	
Project Management Performance	
Most Common Metrics	**Project Alignment with IT Strategy**
% of projects on time, on budget, within scope	% of projects directly linked to business objectives
% of projects compliant with architectural standards	% of applications deployed on a global basis
Customer Satisfaction Index	% of infrastructure standardization projects of total project pool
Project Spending and Costs	% of projects using common project methodology
Actual versus planned ROI for implementation of key initiatives	**% of application failures within first 90 days of deployment**
% of projects with completed business case	% of 'at-risk' projects that adopt quality, security, and compliance standards
% of budget allocated to unplanned projects	Increase in project management maturity
Earned value	Project quality index
Cost Performance Index	
Project Timeliness and Delivery	
% and cost of project rework due to changed scope, poor **requirements definition, etc.**	
Average project duration	
% of projects with detailed project plan	
Dollars saved through productivity improvement and reusable code	
Schedule performance index	
% of project milestones delivered	

Figure 8.5 Composite IT Balanced Scorecard Metrics Used by Representative Best Practice Companies

IT Service Management and Vendor Performance	
Most Common Metrics Key applications and systems availability Help-desk first-call resolution rate	**IT Vendor Management** IT contract cost ($) IT contract cost as a % of IT spend IT project completion (on time, within budget) SLA performance (%) Customer satisfaction index (%)
User-Centric Operational Performance Average number of incidents per user per month (average number of times end user experiences global desktop availability outages per month) Consistently available and reliable IT services to users Rate of failure incidents impacting business	**Help-Desk Performance** Mean time to repair for all network and desktop outages Mean time to repair for all application systems outages less than four hours % of infrastructure service requests closed within service level agreements
Network and Systems Performance Print server availability All critical systems and infrastructure have viable business continuity plans System/application database maintained with more than 95 % accuracy E-mail transmit less than 20 seconds (all regions) Monthly average of network availability consistently more than 99.5 % Monthly average of critical systems availability consistently above 99.5 % Mean time to repair for all client outages less than two hours Network uptime PC/laptop hardware fix or replacement within 48 hours Total cost of ownership of identified products and services compared to industry standards	**Operational Strategy Adoption** Completion of service transformation with minimum business disruption All announced changes completed within advertised downtime window % of IT architectural plans approved, reviewed, and accepted by business Number of applications used by more than one line of business % of desktop PC standardized End-to-end availability for customer service IT effectiveness in resource allocation supporting business objectives Identify and manage strategic alliances with IT partners Decrease average development cost by 10 %
Information Security % of systems compliant with IT security standards Number and type of security incidents time to respond and resolve security incidents	
IT HR Skills Management	
Most Common Metrics Employee morale/satisfaction Overall IT staff retention and attrition rate	**Training and Personal Development** % of performance assessment and development plans delivered to employees % of employees with mentors % of employees with individual development plans % of individual training objectives met Employee 'business knowledge' survey performance % of managers trained in employee motivation % of staff with appropriate measures for their personal goals Share of IT training spent in business units Number of IT person-hours spent at industry events Number of training hours per employee per quarter

Figure 8.5 Composite IT Balanced Scorecard Metrics Used by Representative Best Practice Companies

Staffing	Marketing/ PR - Related Metrics
% of non-entry-level position filled internally	Number of awards won by company for use
Average tenure of solid performers (in years)	of IT
% of projects assignments that are cross-functional	Competitiveness of current employment offer
Ratio of skills sets needed to skills set represented	versus industry
Performance against staff diversity goals	Citation of IT organization in press
Number of candidates interviewed per open position	
IT headcount (number of full-time IT staff)	
Contractor headcount	
% of planned staffing levels	
Average years of IT experience	
% of IT staff who are certified (number of industry recognized certifications)	
Customer Satisfaction	**Customer Satisfaction**
Most Common Metrics	**Most Common Metrics**
Customer satisfaction survey – quarterly or semi-annually	Customer satisfaction survey – quarterly or semi-annually
Surveys	**Surveys**
Overall business executive satisfaction rating	Overall business executive satisfaction rating
Survey Questions	**Survey Questions**
Perceived versus actual price competitiveness of IT services	Perceived versus actual price competitiveness of IT services
Perceived ability to deliver technical/business solutions and services	Perceived ability to deliver technical/business solutions and services
Quality of communication about available services and new technologies	Quality of communication about available services and new technologies
Help-desk client satisfaction—% dissatisfied	Help-desk client satisfaction—% dissatisfied
Contribution to business process improvement and innovation	Contribution to business process improvement and innovation
Contribution to business value creation	Contribution to business value creation
Contribution to corporate business strategy	Contribution to corporate business strategy

Figure 8.5 Composite IT Balanced Scorecard Metrics Used by Representative Best Practice Companies

IT performance, control and compliance framework

A growing number of organizations are using both the COSO and CobiT frameworks as a checklist to develop more effective and complete IT controls. Critical success steps used by several best practice companies to improve controls include:

- establish an IT governance and control framework
- establish management compliance forum
- determine Sarbanes-Oxley and/or other regulatory compliance requirements
- determine IT owners for applications and general controls

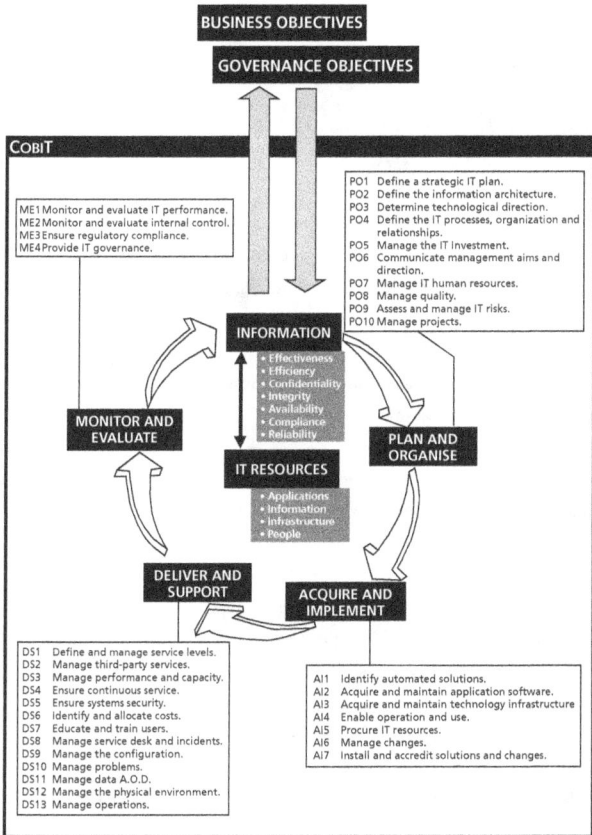

BUSINESS OBJECTIVES

GOVERNANCE OBJECTIVES

COBIT

ME1 Monitor and evaluate IT performance.
ME2 Monitor and evaluate internal control.
ME3 Ensure regulatory compliance.
ME4 Provide IT governance.

PO1 Define a strategic IT plan.
PO2 Define the information architecture.
PO3 Determine technological direction.
PO4 Define the IT processes, organization and relationships.
PO5 Manage the IT investment.
PO6 Communicate management aims and direction.
PO7 Manage IT human resources.
PO8 Manage quality.
PO9 Assess and manage IT risks.
PO10 Manage projects.

INFORMATION
• Effectiveness
• Efficiency
• Confidentiality
• Integrity
• Availability
• Compliance
• Reliability

MONITOR AND EVALUATE

IT RESOURCES
• Applications
• Information
• Infrastructure
• People

PLAN AND ORGANISE

DELIVER AND SUPPORT

ACQUIRE AND IMPLEMENT

DS1 Define and manage service levels.
DS2 Manage third-party services.
DS3 Manage performance and capacity.
DS4 Ensure continuous service.
DS5 Ensure systems security.
DS6 Identify and allocate costs.
DS7 Educate and train users.
DS8 Manage service desk and incidents.
DS9 Manage the configuration.
DS10 Manage problems.
DS11 Manage data A.O.D.
DS12 Manage the physical environment.
DS13 Manage operations.

AI1 Identify automated solutions.
AI2 Acquire and maintain application software.
AI3 Acquire and maintain technology infrastructure
AI4 Enable operation and use.
AI5 Procure IT resources.
AI6 Manage changes.
AI7 Install and accredit solutions and changes.

Source: ITGI

Figure 8.6 COBIT - IT processes by domain

• manage performance, control and compliance issues
• VP-appointed compliance stewards
• VP-appointed applications and controls SME's (subject matter experts)

- design of IT control documentation
- review and audit of IT controls

8.4 Enabling technologies to improve IT governance

There are numerous software tools that enable enterprises to collect, record, analyze, track and report KPIs relating to each IT governance area, but none thus far, that address all of the areas. Several vendors are working on tools that address the enterprise governance processes.

Select technology software solution attributes necessary to support IT governance and its major components:

The following attributes, functions and features, at a minimum, should be included in software packages that support IT governance and its major components:

- **Demand and customer relationship management** – process IT requests, work flow, authorization, accommodate multiple designations (discretionary, mandatory and/or strategic; planned or unplanned; new, enhancements, maintenance and/or 'keep the lights on'), etc.
- **Portfolio management** – investment and alignment evaluation criteria, rankings vis-à-vis alternatives, priorities, approval, etc.
- **Work flow, process management, tracking and authorization**
  - processes, phases and templates (imbedded and/or custom designed), 'go/no go' gates, etc.
- **Planning**
  - link initiatives and track to strategic/tactical/capital/budget plans and initiatives
  - 'what if' alternative analysis
  - work breakdown structure - work package management

- task list
- organization breakdown structure
- estimating and budgeting
- resource loading
- scheduling – multiple techniques

- **Program and project life cycle support** – phases, templates, reviews, authorization, progress tracking and reporting; required to be updated and accessible at multiple levels; ability to link tasks to related tasks and/or projects and/or programs, and record and/or report on multiple key performance indicators – budget, schedule and actuals with variance reporting, status of deliverables, current period, prior period, next period projections, year to date, inception to date, base lining and re-base lining comparisons, etc.

- **Asset management** – inventory of assets, financial value, utilization, aging, depreciation, asset refresh planning, asset retirement and disposal tracking, etc.

- **Configuration management** - asset description, features, costs, location, protocols supported, version and release control, etc.

- **Resource management** – skills inventory, labor rates, labor hours, facilities, inventory, forecasting, level loading, etc.

- **Cost management** – labor rates, procurement rates, committed costs, overhead rates, budget versus actual by labor or procurement category for this period, last period, year to date, inception to date, cost at completion, by product/service, etc.

- **Time management** – from lowest level (activity or tasks) to highest level (project or program), time reporting, budget versus actual comparison by labor or procurement category, etc.

- **Product/service catalogue** – list of standard repetitive IT product and service solutions offered by IT with pricing and estimated deployment time, etc.

- **Financial management** – support capital and expense budgets, cost management, budget and forecasts, accommodate multiple base lines and changes, chargebacks, etc.

- **Performance management** – support and reporting of multiple Balanced Scorecard metrics - planning, project, operational and service performance dashboards, etc.
- **Service level management and support** – incident and problem reporting, tracking and resolution; help desk support; capacity and availability planning and forecasting; usage based tracking, cost allocation, quality control, security, etc.
- **Procurement, vendor, outsourcing management** – link to vendor governance and reporting, contract management, license tracking, metrics, escalation, etc.
- **Compliance management** – documentation, traceability, secure third party access, audit support, etc.
- **Communications management** – manage expectations of customers and constituents - types and frequency of reports, graphs, comparisons, method and frequency of communications supported (e-mail, web-casts, formal reviews, other)
- **Change management** – templates, process, recording, reporting, authorization, original base line and re-base line tracking, version control, etc.
- **Release management** – ensure that all aspects of a new or revised release (eg hardware, software, documentations, checklists and roll-outs) are co-ordinated and approved by the impacted constituents (eg development, operations, client, sponsor, etc.)
- **Issues and problem management** – tracking, reporting and resolution status
- **Security** – access control and authorization data base, authentication, encryption, virus protection, etc.
- **Best practice knowledge management** – maintain a database of internal and external IT governance best practices and continuous improvement ideas and innovations; enable access for select constituents, etc.

8.5 Summary and key take aways

Summary

Each organization should adopt current and emerging industry performance management and control frameworks and models, and tailor them to fit its specific environment. Key points to remember include:
- IT should partner with finance, business and the internal auditors
- align IT objectives, strategies and initiatives with the customer, and develop a set of critical success factors required to meet those objectives – then build key performance indicators to measure performance, and monitor improvement and progress or issues toward those objectives
- identify and prioritize the IT performance management and control policies and procedures, to facilitate compliance, traceability, audit- ability, honesty, security, privacy and control
- make sure that the reward and compensation structure is linked to continuous improvement performance management programs for individuals and teams:
  - provide a link between outcomes and organizational objectives
  - communicate the impact of improvements to all of the stakeholders

Key take aways

The bottom line for each organization is to define, track and enforce those KPIs that measure the CSFs and objectives, and are relevant to the performance management practices and compensation incentives of their enterprises.

IT organizations that gain significant and sustainable improvement in their effectiveness have done so by balancing their focus between the management of IT and the application of IT in the business.

IT managers, who want to build and sustain higher levels of business impact and effectiveness, will implement 'continuous improvement programs' and report 'understandable' results through a robust performance management and control system.

Chapter 9
Summary, lessons learned, critical success factors and future challenges

9.1 Migration plan for making IT governance real and sustainable

IT is an integral part of the business; therefore IT governance must be an integral part of enterprise governance. The following actions are required to achieve a migration to higher levels of IT governance effectiveness and maturity:

- There must be a corporate mandate from the top - the Board and the executive team (including the CIO) are committed to implementing and sustaining a robust governance environment.
- There must be dedicated and available resources - identify executive champion and multi-disciplinary team (to focus on each IT governance component).
- Executives must do their homework – educate on past, current and emerging best practices.
- Executives must market the IT governance value propositions and benefits to the organization - develop and conduct a communications, awareness and public relations campaign.
- A tailored IT governance framework and roadmap must be developed for the organization, based on current and emerging industry best practices.
- An assessment of the 'current state' of the level of IT governance maturity, or other frameworks that relate to specific IT governance components, such as project management, maturity model (PMMM),

vendor management (eSCM), performance management (Balanced Scorecard) and others, as a reference base ('where are we today?'), using a leading industry best practice framework such as CMMI or another framework, that may apply to a specific component of IT governance.

- There must be a 'future state' IT governance blueprint ('where you want to be') developed and kept it in focus.
- There should be activity to decompose the IT governance components into well defined work packages (assign an owner and champion to each process component).
- Executives must develop an IT governance action plan, identify deliverables, establish priorities, milestones, allocate resources and measure progress.
- The organization should sponsor organizational and individual certifications in the IT governance component areas, where they are available (eg PMP, ITIL, IT Security, IT Audit, BCP, Outsourcing, eSCM, COP, etc.).
- There must be activities to identify enabling technologies to support the IT governance initiative.
- There should be a 'web portal' established to access IT governance policies, processes, information, facilitate communications and provide support.
- Celebrate wins.
- Plan for and sustain IT governance process improvements, and link to a reward and incentive structure. Create a 'continuous IT governance improvement group' to sustain the framework.
- Do not focus on specific ROI as a measure of success - use TCO (Total Cost of Operations) and business innovation and transformation metrics as measures of improvement.

9.2 Composite checklist for implementing and sustaining successful IT governance in organizations

This section provides a composite checklist of select best practices identified in the chapters of the book by chapter. It is intended to remind practitioners of the 'must do's' and brings together every critical aspect relating to IT governance in one convenient checklist to help the Board, executive management and, most of all, CIO's and IT professionals, think through what has worked, what can work and how to deploy IT governance successfully.

Chapter 1: Introduction and executive overview

Summary of key strategic, value enhancing and execution questions:

Strategic questions - Is the right thing being done?

Is the investment in IT:

- in line with business vision and strategy?
- consistent with business principles, plan and direction?
- contributing to strategic objectives, sustainable competitive differentiation and business continuity support?
- providing optimum value at an acceptable level of risk?
- representing a long-term view (roadmap)
- including an architectural roadmap, based on a detailed analysis of the current state or condition of IT?

Value Questions – Are the benefits being realized?

Are they:

- delivering a clear and shared understanding and commitment to achieve the expected benefits?
- defining clear accountability, for achieving the benefits which should

be linked to MBOs (management by objectives) and incentive
compensation schemes for individuals and business units or functional
areas?
- based on relevant and meaningful metrics?
- based on a consistent benefits realization process and sign-off?

**Execution Questions – Is the deployment successful and effective?
How are results measured?**

Are they:
- scalable, disciplined and consistent management, governance and
  delivery of quality processes?
- appropriate and with sufficient resources available with the right
  competencies, capabilities and attitudes?
- a consistent set of metrics linked to critical success factors and realistic
  key performance indicators (KPIs)?
- including succession planning?

Purpose and scope of IT governance:

Purpose of IT governance

The purpose of IT governance is to:
- align IT investments and priorities more closely with the business
- manage, evaluate, prioritize, fund, measure and monitor requests for IT
  services, and the resulting work and deliverables, in a more consistent
  and repeatable manner that optimize returns to the business
- provide responsible utilization of resources and assets
- establish and clarify accountability and decision rights (clearly defines
  roles and authority)
- ensure that IT delivers on its plans, budgets and commitments
- manage major risks, threats, change and contingencies proactively
- improve IT organizational performance, compliance, maturity, staff

development and outsourcing initiatives
- improve the voice of the customer (VOC), demand management and overall customer and constituent satisfaction and responsiveness
- manage and think globally, but act locally
- champion innovation within the IT function and business

Scope of IT governance

Key IT governance strategy and resource decisions must address the following topics:

- **IT principles** – high level statements about how IT is used in the business (eg scale, simplify and integrate; reduce TCO (Total Cost of Operations) and self fund by re-investing savings; invest in customer facing systems; transform business and IT through business process transformation; strategic plan directions, PMO (Project Management Office), sustain compliance and other regulatory requirements, etc.)
- **IT architecture** – organizing logic for data, applications and infrastructure captured in a set of policies, relationships, processes, standards and technical choices, to achieve desired business and technical integration and standardization
- **SOA architecture** – service-oriented architecture (SOA) is a business-centric IT architectural approach that supports the integration of the business as linked, repeatable business tasks or services. SOA helps users build composite applications that draw upon functionality from multiple sources within and beyond the enterprise to support business processes
- **IT infrastructure and security** – centrally co-ordinated, based on shared IT services that provide the foundation for the enterprise's IT capability, support and security
- **Business application needs** – specifying the business need for purchased or internally developed IT applications
- **IT investment and prioritization** – decisions about how much and

where to invest in IT (eg capital and expense), including development and maintenance projects, infrastructure, security, people, etc.

- **People (human capital) development** – decisions about how to develop and maintain global IT leadership, management and technical skills and competencies (eg how much and where to spend on training and development, industry certifications, etc.)
- **IT governance policies, processes, mechanisms, tools and metrics** – decisions on composition and roles of steering groups, advisory councils, technical and architecture working committees, project teams; key performance indicators (KPIs); chargeback alternatives; performance reporting, meaningful audit process and the need to have a business owner for each project and investment

Chapter 2: Integrated IT governance framework

Grounded in industry best practice research, and required to plan, develop, deploy and sustain a cost effective approach to IT governance, the blended and integrated governance framework consists of five critical IT governance imperatives (which leverage best practice models described in the chapter and are 'must do's') and address the following work areas:

- **Business strategy, plan and objectives (demand management)** - this involves the development of the business strategy and plan which should drive the IT strategy and plan
- **IT strategy, plan and objectives (demand management)** – this should be based on the business plan and objectives, and will provide the direction and priorities of the IT functions and resources; this should also include portfolio investment management investments, a prioritization scheme and identify the decision rights (who influences decisions and who is authorized to make the decisions) on a wide variety of IT areas, including enterprise architecture; in addition, the CIO is

responsible for the infrastructure investment for such items as capacity planning availability management, security management and related areas.

- **IT plan execution (execution management)** – this encompasses the processes of program and project management, IT Service Management (including ITIL – IT Infrastructure Library and ISO/IEC 20000), risk and continuity management, change management, security, contingency plans and others
- **Performance management and management controls (execution management)** – this includes such areas as the Balanced Scorecard, key performance indicators, CoBIT, and regulatory compliance areas
- **Vendor management and outsourcing management (execution management)** – since companies are increasing their outsourcing spending, selecting and managing the vendors and their deliverables has become critical
- **People development, continuous process improvement and learning** – it is critical to invest in people, knowledge management and sustain continuous process improvement and innovation initiatives

An organization should leverage, adopt and tailor those models, frameworks and/or standards that address those issues, opportunities, pain points and threats most critical to the organization, and create an IT governance roadmap, with clearly defined the roles and responsibilities for IT governance development, process ownership and continuous improvement. The selection of a particular framework or combination of frameworks is largely dependent on the strategic objectives, available resources of an organization and their desired outcomes. All of the frameworks require varying degrees of managing change and cultural transformation.

Chapter 3: Business/IT alignment, strategic/operational planning and portfolio investment management

There are several strategic planning, management control and supplementary principles and practices that, when deployed well, will improve the business and IT alignment environment. They include, but are not limited to, the following:

Strategic planning practices:

This process should be a formal process developed as a partnership and contract (in the loose definition of the word) between the business and IT. It should clearly focus on defining and relating the value that IT provides in support of the business. Specific planning principles and practices should be deployed such as (Selig, 1983):

- **Strategic planning program and processes** - develop a strategic IT plan that is an integral part of the strategic business plan; the plan framework, format and process should be consistent, repeatable and similar, allowing for functional differences between the business units and functions and IT, to facilitate alignment and integration
- **Executive steering committee(s)** - involves top management in the IT/business planning process, to establish overall IT direction, investment levels and approval of major initiatives across the enterprise; each business unit and corporate staff function should have an equivalent body to focus on their respective areas to establish priorities and formalize periodic reviews
- **Investment portfolio management, capital and expense planning and budgeting** – ensures that all IT investments are evaluated, prioritized, funded, approved and monitored using a consistent, but flexible process and a common set of evaluation criteria that are linked to the strategic and annual operating plans and budgets, both capital and expense, at multiple organizational levels

- **Performance management and measurement** – monitors strategic plan outcomes based on specific Balanced Scorecard and service level measurement categories and metrics, and establishes organizational and functional accountability linked to MBO (management by objectives) performance criteria and reviews
- **Planning guidelines and requisites** – a set of general instructions describing the format, content and timing of the business and IT plans; these are general in nature, as opposed to specific standards, and should provide the business units some latitude and flexibility to accommodate local conditions

Management control practices:

These management control practices focus on the tactical and operating plans and programs, and on the day-to-day operational environment:

- **Formalize multi-level IT/business functional/operations/technology steering and governance boards** - with specific roles and decision rights in the day-to-day implementation and Service Management of the tactical IT plans, programs and services
- **Tactical/operating plans and resource allocation** – establishes annual and near term IT objectives, programs, projects and the resources to accomplish the objectives (eg application development plan, infrastructure refresh plan, etc.)
- **Budget/accounting/charge-back** – establishes budgets and monitors expenditures; charges IT costs back to the business or functional users to assure more effective involvement and ownership by the business
- **Performance management and measurement** – collects, analyzes and reports on performance of results against objectives at a more detailed and operational level than at the strategic plan level (see Chapter 8 - Performance Management); in addition, formal periodic monthly and quarterly review meetings should be held to review the status of major initiatives and the on-going performance of IT

Supplementary practices:

These programs will vary by organization that can result in improving alignment:

- **IT/customer engagement and relationship model** - establishes a customer-focused relationship model to facilitate interfaces, decisions, resolution of issues, collaborative plan development, better communications and build trust between IT and the business
- **Program management office (PMO)** – establishes the processes, tools and IT/business unit roles and responsibilities for program and project management; initially, PMOs were established by IT to help manage IT programs and projects; as organizations recognize the increased benefits that a PMO brings to an environment, PMOs are being established at the executive level by a growing number of organizations, to ensure that major corporate business initiatives utilize the same discipline and structure as IT initiatives, to implement them within scope, on-time, within budget and to the customer's satisfaction
- **Marketing, public relations and communications program for IT** – most IT departments are terrible in promoting and marketing their accomplishments and value; developing this function to its full potential creates awareness and promotes executive, management and employee education and commitment to the value of IT, in support of the business through newsletters, websites, press releases, testimonials and other marketing and public relation events
- **IT charter** – promotes effective and definitive interaction and links between the IT and the business/functional groups they support; a charter can provide information on scope, roles and responsibilities, and provide specific program or project authority and limits to that authority
- **Standards and guidelines** – adopt and maintain best practice standards and flexible guidelines to describe and document IT alignment, investment and planning processes, policies and procedures for IT

governance and other areas within IT; for example, a financial services organization developed a simple guideline for its customers entitled, *'How to Request IT Services and Get Them Approved'*, which was a major success

- **Organizational and people development, skills and competencies** – develop a proactive learning environment by encouraging and rewarding education, training and certification (where appropriate)
- **Annual/semi-annual IT management meeting** – conduct periodic IT/ business management meetings, to share best practices, develop stronger relationships, address organizational wide issues and opportunities

Business and IT alignment will remain a major issue in some organizations until they realize that they both need each other to sustain the growth and prosperity of the enterprise.

Chapter 4: Leadership, teams and managing change

Key components of managing large scale enterprise change successfully
As organizations transition to a more mature and effective governance environment, a 'sea change' has to occur, either through incremental and/or radical change that could involve large scale change, depending on an organization's level of maturity, management philosophy and cultural readiness. The four key principles for managing large scale change successfully include (Kotter, 1996):

- engage the top and lead the change –
  - create the 'value proposition' and market the case for change
  - committed leadership
  - develop a plan and ensure consequence management
- cascade down and across the organization, and break down barriers including silos
  - create cross-functional and global teams (where appropriate)

- – compete on 'speed'
- – ensure a performance-driven approach
- mobilize the organization and create ownership
  - – roll-out change initiative
  - – measure results of change (pre-change versus post-change baselines)
  - – embrace continuous learning, Knowledge and best practice sharing
- attributes of effective change teams and agents
  - – strong and focused leader
  - – credibility and authority (charter) to lead the initiative
  - – 'chutzpa', persistent and change zealots
  - – ability to demonstrate and communicate 'early wins' to build the momentum
  - – create a sense of urgency and avoid stagnation
  - – knock obstacles out of the way, diplomatically or otherwise

By applying the above principles to facilitate the transition to a successful IT governance culture and environment, the following steps can be followed:

- **Proactively design and manage the IT governance program**
  – requires executive management sponsorship, an executive champion and creating a shared vision that is pragmatic, achievable, marketable, beneficial and measurable; link goals, objectives and strategies to the vision and performance evaluations
- **Mobilizing commitment, create the guiding coalition and provide the right incentives** – there is a strong commitment to the change from key senior managers, professionals and other relevant constituents; they are committed to make it happen, make it work and invest their attention and energy for the benefit of the enterprise as a whole; create a multi-disciplinary empowered 'Tiger Team' representing all key constituents to collaborate, develop, market and facilitate execution in their respective areas of influence and responsibility

- **Make tradeoffs and choices, and clarify escalation and exception decisions** – IT governance is complex, and requires trade-offs and choices, which impact resources, costs, priorities, level of detail required, who approves choices, to whom are issues escalated etc.; at the end of the day, a key question that must be answered is 'when is enough, enough?'

- **Making change last, assign ownership and accountability** – change is reinforced, supported, rewarded, communicated (the results are through the web and intranet), recognized and championed by owners who are accountable to facilitate the change, so that it endures and flourishes throughout the organization

- **Monitoring progress, common processes, technology and learning** – develop/adapt common policies, practices, processes and technologies, which are consistent across the IT governance landscape and enable (not hinder) progress, learning and best practice benchmarking; make IT governance an objective in the periodic performance evaluation system of key employees and reward significant progress

- **Establish a sense of urgency** – time is money

- **Generate short-term wins** – complete short-term wins that are communicated to the constituents, and are very effective for gaining support and sustaining the change direction

- **Consolidate gains and produce more change** – leverage increased credibility from successes, which facilitates and stimulates the introduction of more change

- **Anchor new approaches in the culture** – institutionalize the process, adapt enabling technology and tools, and link progress to performance

Best practice teams:
Key attributes of best practice teams include:

- clear purpose, common vision and accountability
- obsession with external customer
- participation and well defined roles

- civilized disagreement and style diversity – allow for workout meetings and discussions
- encourage open communications – silence is consent – voice your ideas
- encourage flexible discipline and even expulsion of non-productive team members
- blend of informality and formality
- focus both on process and end results; however, remember that results are more important than process
- acknowledgement of the need for change
- strong respect and trust between members and leaders
- single point of contact for official team progress and communications (do not feed rumor-mill)
- self-assessment of team members and adjustment
- no ideas are bad ideas; encourage no 'blame game'
- use automated tools to increase speed and communications

Chapter 5: Program and project management excellence

Key attributes of a successful program and project based environment
The following principles represent a checklist for helping companies achieve improvements in their program and project management practices and processes:

Program/project management excellence and visibility:
- the CEO (eg CIO; CFO; CMO; COO; etc.) is committed to implementing project management as a core competency to manage all types of projects
- top management must prioritize projects based on a consistent set of evaluation attributes and investment prioritization processes
- customers must approve and set priorities among projects
- implement projects successfully (eg on-time, on-budget, within scope, with high quality and to the customers satisfaction)

- successful project management must be a joint effort between customers and the project teams; but the final responsibility for success or failure lies with the customer in terms of ownership of the results
- market and communicate the benefits and positive results of good fundamental project management disciplines, through newsletters, websites, word of mouth, customer testimonials and other promotion vehicles
- develop a business case for major complex and moderate projects
- an essential element of every project is a complete project plan, based on a work break down structure, with assignable work packages, task identification, estimating, budgeting and scheduling
- planning is everything and on-going – detailed, systematic and team-involved
- what is not documented, has not been said or does not exist
- the more ridiculous the deadline, the more it costs to try to meet it
- project sponsors and constituents must be active participants – this builds relationships, communications and commitment
- use industry standards and guidelines to guide your project management direction - CMMI, PMMM, PMBOK, PRINCE2 and others

Sponsorship and accountability:
- All programs/projects must have a sponsor and/or owner and an overall program/project manager.
- Key roles and responsibilities must be formally agreed to upfront and communicated to all of the constituencies where individuals are assigned specific actions in the form of a **RACI** matrix (**R**esponsible, **A**pprove, **C**onsult, **I**nform) which becomes part of the project documentation.
- Program/project scope, requirements and deliverables should be approved upfront by the sponsor.
- Program/project costs and benefits (including non-financial benefits) should be quantified and approved by the Sponsor and charged back to the sponsor or owner.

- Fast projects have strong leaders who create a sense of urgency and speed.
- Professionalize project management, reward certification and celebrate successes.
- Project Managers must focus on five dimensions of project success
  - on time
  - within budget
  - within scope
  - with acceptable quality
  - to the customer's satisfaction
- Project life cycle with 'go/no go' gates allows for mid-course project reviews and adjustments and/or cancellations.
- A project manager's most valuable and least used word is 'no'.
- Project team members deserve a clear, written charter and guidelines as to the tasks they must perform and the time available to perform them.
- Establish project review panels consisting of key constituents, and conduct formal reviews with follow-up actions, dates and assigned responsibility.
- Use outside subject matter project management experts as needed.

Program/project management (PM) governance:
Key practices for successful and sustainable project management governance include the following:

- A formal project management governance policy should be established defining the components of the policy, and identify what is mandatory and discretionary and who has decision authority for approval, resource allocation, escalation and change authorization.
- A formal governance calendar should be published, which identifies formal project reviews, status reports (eg weekly, bi-weekly, monthly, quarterly), funding reviews, etc.
- A flexible and scalable project management process should be

established and continuously improved, to accommodate different project types such as light, moderate and complex.

- A project management 'center of excellence' (PMO) should be established to develop criteria for project management competencies, encourage project management training and certification, provide expert project management help, act as project management advocates and conduct periodic health checks on select programs/projects.

- Establish a reward and recognition system to recognize project management excellence and encourage certification.

- Deliver short-term incremental project deliverables that work to establish credibility and visibility (decompose complex programs and projects into no more than 80 hour work packages with targeted deliverables, formal project reviews, etc.).

- Incorporate project management objectives into annual performance reviews.

- Consistent program and project metrics should be instituted based on time, cost, resources, quality and customer satisfaction (including earned value, where applicable). There are a number of tools that can help with estimating, resource allocation, level loading and resource utilization.

- Management must be provided with meaningful visibility into projects if suspicion and distrust are to be minimized. The ability to compare planned to actual results or base lines is essential for effective project management.

- The key to good project management is effective and honest communications.

- A formal escalation process, with clear accountability and roles should be established to resolve key program/project issues, risks and approve changes.

- A consistent methodology must be developed and applied to report the **RAG** (eg **R**ed, **A**mber or **G**reen status of programs, projects or other major tasks. Red = significant trouble; Amber = emerging trouble; Green = everything is on target).

- Reporting must be produced on a consistent basis (eg weekly, bi-weekly, monthly, other) using a consistent format (eg with allowances made for the audience of the report).
- A formal time tracking system should be in place to record how time is spent on projects.

Resource optimization, availability and commitment:

- Sponsors and program/project managers should have access to the right resources based on the project phase, and task requirements and competencies needed.
- The availability and commitment of the resources should be guaranteed by senior management once the program/project is approved and resourced.

Program/project management lessons learned:

- Lessons learned should be developed and made available to all constituencies who require them, with consideration given to security and access policies.
- Current and evolving best practice benchmarking should be tracked, adopted and continuously improved.
- Maintain a project management knowledge management system of lessons learned and lessons to be changed.
- Desirable work must be rewarded; undesirable work must be changed.

Chapter 6: IT Service Management

Based on a review of best practice companies, a number of consistent practices seem to be prevalent in these organizations, with regard to superior IT Service Management. They include:

- All steady-state operations (eg PBX, Data Center, Help Desk, Network Management, etc.) must have a primary owner and secondary (back-up) owner.

- The overall ITSM budget should be divided into a set of defined products and services, so that all IT costs can be mapped to supportable business processes, either directly or indirectly.
- All IT services should consistently achieve the desired level of efficiency, productivity, reliability and availability, as measured by the appropriate key performance indicators (eg service level agreements, customer satisfaction, costs, etc.).
- Most IT services should be described as processes that are well documented, consistently performed and repeatable to maximize their efficiency.
- Most ITSM services should be charged back to the user or customer organization to achieve a greater level of accountability.
- The use of an IT service catalogue that can define, price and provide estimated installation time for repetitive productized IT services (eg install a new computer or network connection) is growing in use. It can benefit the customer by providing an easy way to select, order and communicate to IT the required services desired by the customer. The service catalogue does not work for complex, one time initiatives that are not repetitive.
- A formal ITSM governance, reporting and escalation process should be established to resolve key operational issues, risks and conduct periodic reviews. All steady-state operations have business continuity, back-up (including one or more off-site locations), disaster recovery and security policies and procedures.
- All ITSM related processes should be documented in a consistent, repeatable and standard framework, consisting of life cycles, processes and metrics. such as ITIL (IT Infrastructure Library) or ISO/IEC 20000 and be continuously improved.
- Optimizing the utilization of IT assets and resources is critical.

IT Service Management is complex, and requires dedicated resources and leadership to implement effectively. It helps to transition an organization from chaos to order, from a reactive to a proactive environment, from firefighting (most of the time) to a planned environment (with firefighting some of the time), and from random service efforts to predictable and more cost effective service quality. ITIL, much like other IT governance frameworks, represents a journey that is based on a combination of formal life cycle phases, processes and checklists, combined with common sense and managing change proactively.

An IT Service Management initiative does not end after the framework has been implemented. It must be continually monitored, maintained and improved.

Chapter 7: Strategic sourcing, outsourcing and vendor management

Even with the increased outsourcing initiatives in customer organizations, it appears that organizations continue to struggle with establishing and enforcing a more formal, consistent and repeatable outsourcing policy, process and methodology. There are a number of best practice principles and practices that can represent a checklist for helping companies achieve sourcing and outsourcing improvements:

- establishing an appropriate outsourcing strategy, business case and plan
- identifying the appropriate (and prioritizing) the outsourcing opportunities
- developing appropriate approaches and techniques for outsourcing activities
- identifying, selecting and negotiating a 'win-win' deal for service providers
- managing service provider governance and performance management
- managing the transition from the customer to the service provider as a project

- managing the on-going relationship
- conducting periodic formal progress reviews and reports, based on specific metrics relating to the type of outsourcing service or project
- for large initiatives, establishing a high level peer outsourcing governance board for joint reviews
- assigning a service provider account relationship manager as a single point of contact/interface with the customer, and establishing a customer/service provider relationship model

Customer 'to do's':
- executive alignment and commitment to outsourcing that creates a favorable outsourcing culture within the organization
- create a well defined and realistic business case process and case with alternatives
- establish a consistent and formal process for service provider selection and contract negotiations
- develop an outsourcing transition plan from pilot to full implementation, with either re-deployment or termination of displaced resources
- build key performance indicators into the contract performance evaluation system, with both rewards for extraordinary performance and penalties for poor performance
- make KPIs relevant, simple, comparable, easy to report and focused on measurable outcomes
- develop an outsourcing communication plan, risk management and mitigation plan, policy and process
- balance stakeholder needs – companies that successfully outsource continuously 'take the pulse' of all stakeholder groups to adjust their needs over time
- pursue stakeholder involvement on major outsourcing deals, through governance boards, steering committees and working committees
- manage the expectations of all stakeholders well – deliver what you

promise; do not over-promise things you or the outsourcing service provider cannot deliver – credibility is a fleeting attribute that, if lost, is extremely difficult or almost impossible to regain

- experience matters – governance groups can rapidly fill their experience deficit through subject matter expert coaching or outside consulting support
- SLAs are not enough – service-level agreements are extremely important and should be continuously refined and improved over the life of the contract; however, they must be augmented by other methods to ensure customer satisfaction (eg formal and/or informal surveys, listening to the voice of the customer, etc.)
- develop disengagement options and conditions as part of the contract that includes renegotiations options; do not put all of the eggs in one basket
- make sure that a disaster prevention and recovery plan with contingencies is in place

Service provider 'do's':

- understand the expectations of the customer
- communicate your expectations of the customer to the customer
- industry and application knowledge, insight and skills are key
- must be able to scale for volume, capacity, people resources, etc.
- proven methodology, meaningful metrics and performance management reporting
- outline processes and behaviors
- communicate critical information to avoid cultural misunderstandings
- build cross-cultural relationships vital to team success
- use a relationship model with escalation considerations
- have back-up, and recovery plans and facilities

Chapter 8: Performance management and management controls

As part of improving IT governance, it is critical for an organization to establish an overall framework that includes amongst other things, an IT enterprise strategy (which includes business capability roadmaps and Balanced Scorecard metrics), performance management, management controls and compliance components. By using industry best practice frameworks or guidelines, and their components (such as COSO® and COBIT®), a company can develop a more consistent approach to making IT performance management and management controls more effective and sustainable. One needs to assign decision authority, ownership and link deliverables and performance to a reward structure, to make individuals and teams more accountable.

Principles for achieving performance management and management control excellence include:

- identify critical success factors for the business and IT, and identify the key performance indicators (KPIs) linked to these factors
- build key performance indicators into your performance evaluation system, starting at the top and permeating to all positions that can influence those KPIs
- make KPIs relevant, simple, comparable, easy-to-report and focused on goals and objectives
- define and issue a management control policy and related procedures, which identify all of the areas requiring management controls, using COBIT as a checklist
- monitor, audit and ensure that IT operates in accordance with the approved controls
- develop a risk management and mitigation plan, policy and process
- develop a business/IT continuity and disaster recovery plan and policy

- develop a clear performance review, escalation and issues resolution policy and process, with clear accountability and responsibilities
- develop key performance indicators with balance and the 'big picture' in mind (outward from IT to the business and inward to manage IT)
- integrate key performance indicators into individual and team performance evaluation systems
- broad executive commitment – use a mix of business and IT leadership in the design, selection, review and continuous improvement of metrics
- develop standard metrics definition based on consensus
- establish an IT governance and control framework
- establish a management compliance forum
- determine Sarbanes-Oxley and/or other similar regulatory compliance requirements
- determine IT owners for applications and general controls
- manage performance, control and compliance issues

The execution of these plans and objectives must be monitored and measured by a combination of Balanced Scorecard key performance indicators (KPIs), as well as formal and informal status review meetings and reports (eg report cards, dashboards). The outcomes should link critical success factors to KPIs that are measurable, part of a standard reporting system and linked to a governance component. If one cannot measure it, it does not count. Remember, one gets what one measures, so it is critical to measure and control the right things.

9.3 Lessons learned

IT governance is a broad and complex topic, with many parts. IT governance represents a journey. It is not a one time event, and to achieve higher levels of IT maturity, IT governance should be persistently and relentlessly pursued, both from a top-down and a bottom-up perspective.

Creating and sustaining a more effective IT governance environment will take time and resources, and should be focused on achieving incremental IT governance successes in priority areas, based on their value proposition or reduction of major 'pain point' to the organization.

It is critical to break down or segment the IT governance initiative into manageable, assignable and measurable components, or work packages with targeted deliverables. It is important to define clear roles for the board, executive management and the IT governance project team, including ownership and accountability for each component and the overall initiative.

Based on the extensive research and case studies, the major lessons learned to be successful in implementing a successful IT governance initiative must:

- have corporate mandate from the top
- have dedicated and available resources
- recognize that 80 to 90% of an IT governance initiative represents a 'cultural change', and organizations must prepare for a lengthy and involved period of adjustment
- use a phased approach to implement new processes and enabling technologies
- develop and conduct a marketing, communications and awareness campaign focus on value propositions
- create a 'continuous IT governance improvement group', to sustain the momentum, be advocates, act as change agents and sustain the framework and components
- use 'total cost of operations' as a measure of improvement from the current state baseline to the future state baseline

9.4   Critical success factors

Critical success factors for achieving IT governance excellence:

- Create the right environment and culture:
    - establish the appropriate organizational mindset, culture and environment
    - obtain executive sponsorship, commitment and multi-level management buy-in and ownership
    - establish an IT executive governance steering committee and working committee with clearly defined roles and responsibilities
    - success depends on creating a sustainable foundation (eg policy, process, metrics) for managing programs and projects, and integrating results and methodologies into the culture of the organization
    - define roles and get the right people involved in phase
    - market and re-enforce (eg training, rewards, mentors, tools, flexible processes) the value and benefits of good IT governance practices
    - understand the risks, constraints and obstacles and develop contingency plans and actions
    - adopt a flexible and scalable IT governance process (phases, templates, repository, tools and tailor when required) to accommodate different levels of maturity and organizational styles

- Develop an IT governance implementation plan:
    - define the project's charter and boundaries including scope, objectives, requirements and deliverables
    - establish well-defined phases/tasks, 'go/no go' gates and milestones (break the job down into manageable work packages – '80 hour' rule) with realistic baselines (costs, time, resources and contingencies) based on short term incremental and visible deliverables
    - define a responsibility assignment matrix – Responsible, Inform, Consult and/or Approve

  – establish formal change management and risk management processes
  – establish and assess current baseline in terms of costs, resources, competencies, documentation, levels of maturity and identify gaps
  – define the future desired or targeted baseline

- Ensure governance and excellent communications:
  – establish a governance, control, reporting and escalation policy and process
  – manage expectations of all stakeholders proactively
  – identify, measure and track mandatory and discretionary vital signs, metrics, key issues and take necessary actions quickly – knock obstacles out of the way
  – establish frequent and open communications with stakeholders (both formal and informal review meetings) on a daily, weekly, monthly and quarterly basis depending on the project's importance and closeness to being implemented
  – ensure accurate, timely and meaningful monitoring and progress reporting

- Institutionalize and operationalize IT governance
  – create IT governance 'centers of excellence' (eg Advocacy Center, Help Desk, Education, Training, Subject Matter Expert Help, Process, Project Tracking, Certification, Website, etc.)
  – create a reward and/or recognition policy to re-enforce and sustain
  – conduct formal program/project reviews
  – develop and use consistent, flexible and scalable processes (eg fast track or light versus complex projects) and automate processes and tools (web-based)
  – capture and apply lessons learned, and focus on continuous improvement

www.ingramcontent.com/pod-product-compliance
Lightning Source LLC
Chambersburg PA
CBHW032329210326
41518CB00041B/1982